IR

"The gripping story of a crime and an er
both a good story and a valuable history lesson."

—Richard D. Lamm, former governor of Colorado

"Dick Kreck has done it again! With the skills of a first-rate reporter, he explores the many facets of a little-known piece of Colorado history and in the process sheds light on Colorado's early justice system. *Anton Woode* is a fascinating read that takes you into the past and, at the same time, provides a chilling look at the present."

—Margaret Coel, *New York Times* best-selling
author of *The Eye of the Wolf*

"Dick Kreck once again writes a triumph and a real tour de force. ... We follow the eleven-year-old through murder, court trials, imprisonment, jail breaks, and battles with parole boards and the juvenile justice system. It's a riveting story told by a master storyteller."

—David Halaas, former chief historian at the Colorado
Historical Society and author of *Halfbreed:
The Remarkable True Story of Geo*   *Bent*

"A fascinating look at juvenile justice at the turn of the twentieth century and its tireless reformer Ben Lindsey. What became of Anton Woode, the youngest murderer in Colorado history, is a compelling argument for why children should not be treated as adults."

—Stephanie Kane, author of the
best seller *Seeds of Doubt*

"[Dick Kreck] takes a fascinating but little-remembered piece of our local history—this one a mix of murder mystery, courtroom drama, frontier prison life, and juvenile justice at the end of the nineteenth century—researches it with the care of an experienced historian and journalist, and then tells the tale with the sensibility of a gifted storyteller."

—Stephen White, *New York Times* best-selling author
(from the foreword)

"Kreck offers an inviting…historical window on the still burning issue of how to treat juvenile criminals."

—*Publishers Weekly*

Also by Dick Kreck

Murder at the Brown Palace:
A True Story of Seduction and Betrayal

Denver in Flames:
Forging a New Mile High City

Colorado's Scenic Railroads

Anton Woode

Anton Woode
The Boy Murderer

Dick Kreck

Fulcrum Publishing
Golden, Colorado

Text copyright © 2006 Dick Kreck

Library of Congress Cataloging-in-Publication Data
Kreck, Dick.
  Anton Woode : the boy murderer / Dick Kreck.
    p. cm.
  Includes bibliographical references.
  ISBN 1-55591-578-7 (pbk.)
  1. Woode, Anton. 2. Murderers—Colorado—Biography. 3.
Murder—Colorado. I. Title.
  HV6533.C6K74 2006
  364.152'3092—dc22

                                  2006002637
ISBN-13: 978-1-55591-578-0
ISBN-10: 1-55591-578-7
Printed in the United States of America by Thomson-Shore, Inc.
0 9 8 7 6 5 4 3 2 1

Editorial: Faith Marcovecchio, Katie Raymond
Design: Jack Lenzo
Cover image: Courtesy of Colorado Historical Society,
Mazzulla Collection, FF865, Box 13 (detail)

Fulcrum Publishing
16100 Table Mountain Parkway, Suite 300
Golden, Colorado 80403
(800) 992-2908 • (303) 277-1623
www.fulcrumbooks.com

For the only Mother I have

Contents

Acknowledgments

My first and greatest thanks go to researcher Lou-Jean Holland Rehn, who used genealogy magic to track down the final days of Anton Woode. I spent a year and countless hours trying find the elusive fellow, only to be stymied by his sudden disappearance from Menomonie, Wisconsin, in 1923. Without her tenacity and her skill mining public records, there literally would have been no satisfactory ending to the story.

There are others, of course. LaDonna Gunn and Sue Cochran of the Local History Center of the Cañon City Public Library and Pat Kant of the Museum of Colorado Prisons in Cañon City were always ready and willing to dig into their archives for answers to obscure questions about Woode's life in prison.

As they always are, members of the staff at the Western History and Genealogy Department of the Denver Public Library were exemplary, particularly Bruce Hanson, who taught me a lot about Colorado history and researching missing persons through the Internet. It was Karyl Klein at the Colorado Historical Society who unearthed from the society's vast Fred Mazzulla Collection the cover photograph, thought lost, of young Anton Woode and his bigger-than-life musket.

My friend Connie M. Ross by happenstance was living in Wisconsin and took on the task of burrowing into Anton Woode's life there, unearthing some very useful information that filled many gaps. And she trekked to Minneapolis to search out, clean up, and photograph his last resting place in, as she described it, her "interview suit."

Pat Favata of the Newburgh (New York) Historical Society became as excited as I when we first talked about The Boy Murderer and doggedly pursued Woode's life in the Hudson Valley and his connections and family in the community. It was Jim White of the Denver office of Volunteers of America who ferreted out information and rare photographs of Maud Ballington Booth, "the little mother of the prisons," who helped turn around Woode's life.

David Wetzel of the Colorado Historical Society not only read the manuscript with the eye of an English teacher, which he was, and an editor, which he is, but the subject of the book was his idea. Having read *Murder at the Brown Palace*, he said to me over beers one day, "If you like murder so much, you should look at this young man named Anton Woode, who shot and killed his hunting partner for his pocket watch." He launched the search.

And one is always indebted to those with the patience to read an unedited manuscript and the courage and enthusiasm to suggest changes. Among them were David F. Halaas, Victoria Heath, Beth Hendrix, Ed Will, and Bob Rector, my friend since high school, who rightly felt free to say anything.

Writing a book is one thing. Producing it is another. I was fortunate to have the skilled presence at Fulcrum Publishing of Faith Marcovecchio, who made suggestions that, without bruising my authorial ego, made the story more fast-moving and complete, and Jack Lenzo, who did the design work.

Thank you all.

Foreword

On the day he was charged as an adult in the first-degree murder of Taylor DeMarco, Eric Stoneman probably had clear memories of blowing out the candles on his fourteenth birthday cake.

Stoneman made history with his crime: he became one of the youngest children ever to be charged with homicide as an adult in Colorado.

Eric Stoneman is, however, *not* the boy murderer in Dick Kreck's new book.

Instead, Eric Stoneman's story is one of the tragic reasons that Dick Kreck's new book is so timely and important.

———

When Dick Kreck approached me about writing the foreword for *The Boy Murderer* and briefly explained what it was about, I was more than a little intrigued. My interest was piqued for a couple of reasons, one perhaps more surprising than the other.

The unsurprising reason is that I was honored to be asked.

The Boy Murderer is what we've come to expect from Dick Kreck. In it, he takes a fascinating but little-remembered piece of our local history—this one is a mix of murder mystery, courtroom drama, frontier prison life, and juvenile justice at the end of the nineteenth century—researches it with the care of an experienced historian and journalist, and then tells the tale with the sensibility of a gifted storyteller.

Dick Kreck has long provided another service to our community too. He is one of a small cadre of local writers—Tom Noel and John Dunning come to mind as well—who are intent on insisting that Denver not forget the details, many of them sordid and less than flattering, of the Queen City's relatively short, colorful history. Kreck is equally intent on not permitting contemporary residents of Denver the luxury of pretending that our city's history is one that took place only in ranch house parlors, or Denver mansion drawing rooms, or in courtrooms graced by western gentility and frontier manners. His books remind us that Denver's growing pains as a city, and as a society, were often unseemly, and he holds up a well-placed mirror to let us see how we've been doing recently by comparison.

Readers of Dick Kreck's previous book, *Murder at the Brown Palace*, were treated not only to a captivating journalistic account of one of early-twentieth-century Denver's most infamous crimes of passion, but also to an unadulterated look at the often-indecorous nature of urban Colorado life in the years prior to World War I. *Murder at the Brown Palace* is very much a captivating murder mystery, but in Dick Kreck's hands, the story is also a morality tale about the prejudices that were part of the fabric of Denver society and of the inequities that were an accepted part of the political and judicial systems in Colorado government.

Readers will be rewarded with nothing less in *The Boy Murderer*.

The second, more surprising reason for my immediate interest in *The Boy Murderer* was because I recognized that the unlikely events in Kreck's account of what had happened to one child in the Denver that existed just as the nineteenth century was becoming the twentieth seemed to be replaying themselves at the precise time that he mentioned his book to me. Here we were, smack in the middle of the first decade of the twenty-first century, and Colorado jurisprudence was struggling with almost the exact same problems in juvenile justice that Kreck's account chronicles from a century before.

Precisely 100 years after Anton Woode—Woode *was* the boy murderer of Kreck's book, and Colorado's youngest-ever murderer convicted as an adult—was released from his twelve years of incarceration in the Colorado State Penitentiary, a modern case was developing in Colorado that seemed to underscore how little evolution had occurred in our state regarding the provision of appropriate criminal justice to juveniles.

In Glenwood Springs, in July 2005, 9th Judicial District Attorney Colleen Truden reached a controversial determination that yet another accused child murderer, a boy named Eric Stoneman, should be charged as an adult in the first-degree murder of one of his playmates, Taylor DeMarco.

Eric Stoneman had just turned fourteen.

Compared to Anton Woode, though, Eric Stoneman was an old man.

Anton Woode, the boy murderer in Dick Kreck's book, had been eleven old—yes, eleven—when he was convicted of murder in 1893 and sentenced to the Colorado State Penitentiary.

What have we learned in the interim?

I think you'll find yourself asking the same question as you digest Dick Kreck's dramatic recounting of the troubling story of Anton Woode, as you try to understand the grim circumstances that led to the vicious crime he committed, as you try not to be appalled by his subsequent treatment by the courts, and as you try—unsuccessfully, I will wager—not to be horrified by his experiences as a child in the state penitentiary. I think, like me, you'll wonder, too, what on earth happened to the all the progressive changes that were being promoted by the juvenile justice reformers who came to Anton Woode's defense at the time.

And after you read *The Boy Murderer* and you think about Eric Stoneman, or the next child offender who gets muscled into the adult criminal justice system, I think you'll wonder how Colorado could have made so little progress in so many years.

Dick Kreck's *The Boy Murderer* should be unforgettable. Unfortunately, history says it may not be. Judge for yourself. You'll be glad you did.

—Stephen White

1

Chapter One

Anton Woode was at that awkward age—too old to set free, too young to hang.

As he sat behind his lawyer at the defendant's table in the courtroom, no one who looked at the sweet-faced boy could believe that he was guilty of what he was on trial for—shooting a man in the back. He was, after all, only eleven years old, if his mother were to be believed.

The blond, blue-eyed boy had the face of an angel, or would have had it not been for his out-sized ears, which stuck straight out from either side of his head. Those crowded into the courtroom strained to get a look at the child the newspapers branded "The Boy Murderer." He was so tiny, about four foot eight, his feet barely reached the floor as he sat in his chair.

The facts presented at the trial were simple. Woode was out hunting rabbits near his family's farm in the bleak gully country near Brighton, Colorado, north of Denver, on a crisp early November day in 1892. Hunting was one of the few enjoyments Woode had. That, and dipping into his father's beer stash almost every Saturday while the latter was away on business. He didn't go to school regularly—it was too far away—although he was fond of Sunday school. He'd never been to Denver, even though it was only twenty miles south.

Anton was an excellent shot, despite the fact that his weapon, almost as tall as he, was an ancient musket with its broken stock held together by copper wire. He usually hit what he aimed for.

That same morning, November 2, 1892, three friends—Alexander Baker, Harry Wyman, and Joseph Smith—set out in a wagon from Denver at about 4 A.M. on a duck-hunting expedition. The trio set up camp and started hunting at about eight in the morning, but by midday they had had little success, so they decided to split up. Wyman walked off by himself while Smith and Baker secured the horses near an abandoned ranch. It was then that

lit—11+
12. yrs old

this is the gun *that Killed Smith*

Young Anton Woode holds the battered musket with which he gunned down Joseph Smith from behind in November 1892. The ancient weapon, nearly as tall as Woode, was held together with copper wire, and his rough clothing is a testament to his impoverished upbringing. Someone later wrote at the bottom of the photograph, "This is the gun that killed Smith."

they met Anton Woode, who appeared suddenly from behind a building.

"Do you own this wagon and horses?" Woode asked Baker.

"No."

"What time is it?"

"I have no watch."

"Well, you don't seem to own anything."

"No, I don't have anything but my gun."

Smith, meantime, worked his way into a small ravine. Woode and Baker hurried to catch up with him, scaring up a rabbit that scampered into a group of horses standing in a pasture.

"Why don't you shoot?" Woode said to Baker.

"I don't want to shoot and hit one of the horses."

"Oh, never mind; them horses don't belong to nobody. They've been around here all summer."

When the rabbit cleared the horses, Baker shot and killed it. Woode wanted it, but Baker refused to give it up.

They heard a shot not far away, and when they caught up with Smith, they found him using a length of wire to extract a rabbit from a hole it had run into before dying. As Smith fished for the rabbit, Woode asked him what time it was. Smith pulled his gold watch out of a pocket. Woode's eyes glittered.

Woode told Smith that he knew where the rabbits "were thicker than the hairs on his head." Being only a mile from his house, Woode was familiar with the country.

To a visitor, there wasn't much to recommend the place. It was flat, arid, and laced with gullies and washes, not good for much but, thanks to irrigation, raising sugar beets and a few dairy cows. For Woode, the desolate area west of town toward the Rocky Mountains was his playground, a chance to escape his dull, hardscrabble life on the farm, and a place to hunt rabbits. Baker had no interest in rabbits, he was after ducks, so he went his own way and rejoined his friend Wyman while Smith followed Woode in the opposite direction. It was about 2:30 in the afternoon. Baker and Wyman walked less than a hundred yards when they heard two shots and looked back to see that Smith had brought down another rabbit. Minutes later, they heard another shot, but by then Woode and Smith were out of view.

Later that afternoon, Baker and Wyman waited by the wagon, where the three men had agreed they would make camp and resume hunting in the morning. Smith didn't return. When it turned 6 P.M. and twilight began to fade, Baker and Wyman agreed that they'd better search for their friend. They circled the last place they saw Smith and fired their guns into the air, hoping to attract his attention. After a three-hour search that they estimated covered about five miles, they gave up. It was pitch black.

Early the next day, Baker and Wyman set off again. Before long, less than 200 yards off a curve in the road through the small foothills, they found Smith's body on a hillside, not far from where Baker last saw him alive. He was lying face up, his eyes wide open, staring sightless at the sky. His feet were close together, his arms flung straight out to either side. They knew he was beyond help. "The cold stare on his face and the ashen hue of his flesh at once showed us that he was dead," Baker later told the *Rocky Mountain News*. The two men were reluctant to disturb the crime scene, but Baker checked the dead man's pockets and discovered that his gold watch and chain were missing.

Baker and Wyman hurried back to Denver and, at 4:30 that afternoon, reported the shooting to the Arapahoe County coroner, John M. Chivington, the same man vilified for leading his troops into a slaughter of Indian women and children at Sand Creek in 1864. Late the next day, Baker returned to the scene with Chivington and deputy sheriffs Bert Holloway and T. J. Thompson. Chivington later recalled seeing "the bleak hills stretching out everywhere, the grim mountains off in the distance, and the pale blue light from the moon shining down on the snow." They quickly found Smith's body, still undisturbed, and they noticed footsteps in the snow leading away from the crime scene.

Curiously, there was no blood to be seen on the body. When the deputies turned him over, they saw why. A single ball had entered Smith's body just under the right shoulder blade. The impact caused him to spin around and land on his back. As the wound bled, Smith's blood saturated the sandy soil beneath him.

Woode, last seen walking away to go hunting with Smith, immediately became a suspect.

Chapter Two

Satisfied that Joseph Smith was the victim of a single fatal gunshot in the back, Alexander Baker, Bert Holloway, T. J. Thompson, and a fourth man, George Duggan, shared a horse-drawn rig and followed footprints in the snow from the scene of the shooting to the Woode farm less than a mile away.

In a ploy to gain entry to the house, they asked for supper and feed for their horses but were turned away by Anton's mother, Maggie Woode. The men drove their wagon about a half mile away, walked back to the farmhouse, and knocked again. When Mrs. Woode answered, they told her their real purpose for coming. She told them Anton wasn't home, that he was gone to school in Elyria, down near

Denver. They didn't believe it and searched the house. There, hiding beneath his bed, was the terrified Woode. Thompson grabbed the boy by his leg and pulled him out.

"What have you done with Smith's watch?" one of the men asked.

Slowly, silently, Anton reached into his pocket and withdrew the shiny gold watch that he had so coveted.

"Where's the chain?"

Without a word, he pulled it out too.

There was no sign of Smith's shotgun. Woode told the deputies that his father had taken it, but further searching revealed it hidden between the mattresses on Anton's bed.

Thompson and Holloway took the boy outside. "Why'd you kill him?" Holloway asked gently.

Woode didn't hesitate, saying that he did it for Smith's watch. "I've never had anything nice. I wanted it."

As they walked and talked, Holloway asked Woode if he could show him where the shooting took place. Guileless, the boy said, "Yes, come along with me." He took the bulky deputy's hand and led him to within a few feet of where Smith's blood darkened the ground. Woode told the men that when he got home, he told his father what he had done and his father told him to keep quiet about it. Later, he said, they planned to bring the body to the farm and bury it. Thompson and Holloway had heard all they needed to. They arrested Woode and his parents, the latter for lying about Woode's whereabouts and for their complicity in events following the shooting.

Two days later, as Woode slept on his cot in the Arapahoe County Jail, he was visited by Richard Wells, a reporter for *The Colorado Sun*. "Sleeping sweetly and soundly," he was gently shaken awake by Mrs. James Havens, the matron assigned to take care of him. He confessed everything. Wells, like a prosecuting attorney, hammered at the sleepy boy with a middle-of-the-night interrogation, then wrote about it on page one of his newspaper.

"Anton, did you kill Joe Smith?"
"Yes."
"Why did you do it?"
"'cause."
"Did you quarrel with him?"
"Yes."
"About what?"
"Oh, sumfin."

Joseph Smith, hunting with two friends near Brighton, Colorado, was last seen alive walking away with Anton Woode on November 2, 1892. He was found dead the next day, a single shot in his back, his gold pocket watch and shotgun missing.

The Denver Times/Courtesy Colorado Historical Society, OEH 498

"The rabbits?"

"Yes."

"Why did you take his watch?"

"I wanted it."

"Was it a pretty watch?"

"Yes!"

"Did you ask him for it?"

"Yes."

"And he wouldn't give it to you?"

"No, so I shot him in the back."

"What did he do when you shot him?"

"He jes' turned and looked at me and fell."

"Did your father tell you to shoot him?"

"No."

"What were you going to do with the body?"

"I was going to take it and bury it."

"How were you going to do that?"

"I was going to get a horse and carry it up in front of our house and bury it."

"Are you sorry you killed Joe?"

"Yes, I'm sorry."

While others were mired in disbelief, Coroner Chivington had no doubt that Woode planned and executed the shooting out of greed, and Chivington happily shared his theory with *The Sun*.

> There is something in the surroundings of this youth, Woode, that tended to make him as he is. He was born out there amid the rough, bleak hills. The boy has simply partaken of the surroundings. He is physically sapped and morally barren. He never had anything nice himself; he saw the poor murdered lad with a beautiful watch; he coveted it, and the price seemed cheap to him. It was only a lad who stood in the way of his possession of what every boy most wants, a watch and a gun.

Smith was gone off with the angels less than a week when law-enforcement officials, ministers, and alienists (a nineteenth-century term for psychiatrists) began to debate the heinous nature of Anton Woode's crime, trying to penetrate behind those bright blue eyes and determine what led one so young to commit such a brutal act.

An anonymous letter writer who signed his editorial in the *Rocky Mountain News* "X.Y.Z." offered an explanation of the youngster's behavior:

To one who has psychologically studied the mind of a child and knows what effect environment and daily example have on the nature of the impressible little mortal, the amazement is that there is only one Anton Woode in the community instead of many in each neighborhood. In each little human being that comes into the world is the latent germ of savagery—survival of the time when his ancestors were constantly obliged to take life, either as a means of self-preservation or to obtain the necessities of living.

What shall we do to keep this latent spark of savagery undeveloped till it withers away from disuse? What we usually do is to awaken and develop it. We put cap pistols into the hands of our four-year-olds and play at letting them shoot us falling over most realistically.

A little later we give the boy a nickle-plated and joint shotgun, for throwing missiles of some kind, and valuable to him because it "looks like a real one." The mind surely grows by what it feeds on. It is a pitiful and distressing but perfectly logical result.

The five-and-dime psychoanalysis was the first glimmer of young Woode's defense—that he was too young to know the difference between right and wrong—and it was also the beginning of a meandering legal road leading eventually to courts holding parents legally responsible for their child's behavior.

Chapter Three

A popular opinion at the turn of the twentieth century was that juvenile criminals are born, not made. A veteran police officer told the *Rocky Mountain News* in 1901, "A tendency to be a criminal, the commission of crime, on the part of man, is the simple outcome of those traits of character implanted in the superior animal by nature."

It might be, said one "expert," the result of genetics. Police were happy to cite the notorious Gavin clan of hoodlums in which criminal behavior became a family business. Charles Gavin arrived in Denver in the early 1890s, and for ten years, he and his three sons were constant visitors to the police blotter. Their legacy among local law enforcement was that a criminal most often looked like a criminal, distinguished by a bullet-shaped head, eyes set too close together, and an extended chin.

Fair-haired and baby-faced, Woode did not fit the "criminal" description, but, *The Denver Republican* intoned, "In the criminal history of America there have been been few crimes that compare in any way in the amount of depravity with that shown in the killing of Joe Smith by eleven-year-old Anton Woode." It was, proclaimed *The Colorado Sun*, " ... the most cold-blooded crime in the history of the state of Colorado."

Today, childhood at the turn of the twentieth century is viewed as an idyllic time. But for many children of the late 1800s, life was harsh. Crimes, petty and capital, more often were the result not of genetics but of children left to fend for themselves in an era when early death was not unheard of among young mothers. Alcohol and neglect ravaged many families. Fathers who worked twelve-hour days and soothed themselves with frequent trips to the neighborhood watering hole many times were not around to keep an eye on their offspring. "Nine of ten cases of juvenile delinquency are caused by the fact that the home has been broken up because one of the parents was an habitual drunkard," Mrs. Ida L. Gregory, a clerk in the juvenile court, declared in *The Denver Post* in 1912.

On the other hand, Dr. Pearl Wheeler Dorr, who, *The Post* said, made a ten-year study of "feeble-minded" students in the Denver public schools, believed the principal cause lay elsewhere. "The greatest cause of mental and physical wreckage is the fact that our American children are overfed with excitement. When they become restless at home they are given a nickel to go to the five-cent shows. If they crave stimulants they are allowed to drink coffee at will and learn to use alcohol at a very early age. As a result, the nervous system is broken down and the next generation is feeble-minded."

Childhood diseases such as mumps, polio, smallpox, diphtheria, and tuberculosis cut many young lives short, but the medications used to treat these ailments were often more life-threatening than the diseases. Alcohol- and drug-laced palliatives with upbeat names such as "Mother's Helper" and "Infant's Quietness," potions based on a powerful drug called laudanum, a potent combination of alcohol and opium, were fed to fussy babies to quiet them.

Anton Woode's impoverished, liquor-laced life out in the country was enough to lead any boy into a life of crime, but children in the city were even more at risk. They often wandered the streets of Denver, frequenting the gambling houses, houses of prostitution, and saloons that lined Curtis and Market Streets in the city's lower districts. Their delinquencies included stealing, assault and battery, sexual promiscuity, truancy, cursing, smoking cigarettes, and "bad associations." In 1883, there were an estimated forty public gambling houses operating around the clock, even on Sundays. Young girls fresh off the train at Denver's Union Station at the foot of 17th Street were particularly easy prey for recruiters for the city's houses of prostitution, located only blocks from the depot. Even historian William Vickers's generally fawning 1880 *History of the City of Denver, Arapahoe County and Colorado* expressed embarrassment over the wide-open district, noting, "Denver, it must be confessed, is sadly deficient in places of legitimate amusement, though concert halls are unhappily only too plenty in the lower part of the city." These so-called "concert halls" were little more than high-class saloons featuring gambling and prostitutes.

Fighting the Traffic in Young Girls, a melodramatic tale of the horrors of the white-slave trade written in 1910, warned, "I cannot escape the conclusion that the country girl is in greater danger from the 'white slavers' than the city girls. That is because they are less sophisticated, more trusting and more open to the allurements of those who are waiting to prey upon them." Further, it noted ominously, "The danger begins the moment a girl leaves the protection of Home and Mother." Tom Noel described in his landmark history *The City and the Saloon* how investigators entered a wine room in the lower precincts and found "a woman playing with a dog in an obscene manner" and, in the same shop, "a little girl about twelve years old" being held up by her heels and spanked by a group of men.

In his *Hell's Belles*, a history of prostitution in Denver, Clark Secrest described "talent scouts," men and women who ranged throughout the city, sometimes in the unlikeliest of venues. "Ice cream parlors and sidewalk fruit stands, innocent as they might sound, were important recruiting stations for youthful, properly dressed, and sincere-sounding recruiters ... because these were natural and seemingly innocent places for a young girl to stop during her first days in the new city." These recruiters ranged far and wide, trolling for gullible young women at amusement parks, dance halls, five-cent movie houses, traveling theater companies, gambling parlors, and wine rooms, the last nothing more than glorified saloons that catered to a female clientele. Even divorce courts, where young, unskilled women sometimes were left without financial support, were fertile hunting grounds.

The story of Addie Bayman, fifteen and "well-developed for her years," according to *The Post*, was not atypical. Her slide into a life of degradation began, she said, when she visited a chile parlor next to Pennington's Saloon on Curtis Street. There, she said, "I met George Graff and a man whose name I don't know, but who owned the chile parlor. They wanted me to go into Pennington's wine room and I said no at first, but they coaxed me so hard that I went along. That was the first time I ever was in a wine room and I drank some beer. Well, I just started going around and I met a lot of men at dances, who used to take me out, and that's the way it started."

Boys, some as young as seven or eight years old, were vulnerable as well. Newsboys, for example, hustled papers or shined shoes on street corners, and it was first come, first served for the most profitable locations. Boys slept in hotel lobbies, vestibules, doorways, or under benches in the train depot rather than go home, so that they could be first in line to get their papers and the best corners early the next morning. In the mid-1890s, the city issued badges to newsboys, indicating that they were licensed to sell papers, thus ending the rush to grab corners before their young rivals got there. It brought some order to the chaos.

Children from the lower classes and immigrant homes, both of which paralleled Woode's young life, were particularly at risk. Their families were frequently torn apart by alcohol addiction, unemployment, illness, and abandonment. If they couldn't carry their economic weight at home, wherever that might be, children were considered liabilities and abandoned to make their own way. They became "street children," forced to live on a few pennies a day by selling newspapers or matches or getting by by stealing, which often resulted in jail time.

"One of the greatest difficulties with Denver boys, and I think with boys generally, is idleness," Judge Benjamin B. Lindsey, founder of Denver's Juvenile Court in 1903 and regarded as one of the founding fathers of juvenile law in America, wrote in *The Post* in 1904. "If not employed at some useful thing they are generally on the streets or in alleys, the downtown poolrooms and bowling alleys, engaged not always in wholesome play, but

Boys and girls, some as young as seven years old, were forced by abuse at home, economic circumstance, or neglect to try to earn a living on Denver's streets. This group of young news hawks stands next to *The Denver Post* in about 1900, hoping for a chance to earn a few pennies on one of the city's contested street corners.

Dick Kreck collection

too often in the most demoralizing character of dawdling, idling, cigarette smoking and dirty-story telling, with absolutely no thought of work or the serious side of life."

Laws made no distinction between juvenile and adult crime. Any crime, no matter how petty, could result in jail time. City jail was a breeding ground of crime and criminals. In Lindsey's view, it was a cesspool of "filth and vermin and all its vileness, into which over two thousand Denver boys, between ten and sixteen years of age, were thrust. ... " Though their crimes were tossed into a common basket, young offenders sometimes were sent to reformatories, little more than hard-labor camps where inmates slaved until they were judged "reformed" or reached their twenty-first birthday.

Lindsey did not view young criminals as inherently flawed, and said so in his landmark *The Beast*:

> Children are neither good or bad, but either weak or strong. They are naturally neither moral or immoral but merely unmoral. They are little savages, living in a civilized society that has not yet civilized them, often at war with it, frequently punished by it, and always secretly in rebellion

against it, until the influences of the home, the school and the church gradually overcome their natural savagery and make them moral and responsible members of society.

Whether Woode was to become "a moral and responsible" member of society would be decided at his trial in Denver for murder, which began on February 27, 1893. The verdict seemed predetermined. He'd already confessed twice.

Chapter Four

DAY ONE, FEBRUARY 27, 1893

Shortly before 10 A.M. on Monday, February 27, 1893, Anton Woode made his first court appearance. Every head in the jammed courtroom turned as one when Deputy Sheriff Tom Clark walked his small prisoner into Judge David V. Burns's court in the Arapahoe County Courthouse, which stood at the corner of 16th Street and Court Place until it was demolished in 1934. The boy's eyes darted around the room, taking in the trappings of a drama he couldn't begin to comprehend.

Some of those in attendance gasped when they got their first look at the boy whose blond hair was neatly combed, his face newly scrubbed. He looked like anything but a murderer, one who cold-bloodedly shot down the unsuspecting Joe Smith for his pocket watch. Instead, noted one observer, he looked like "a golden-haired, blue-eyed country boy." Another thought he should be given a severe spanking and hauled off to an institution.

Amid the courtroom turmoil, Anton calmly took his place behind attorney John A. Deweese, who, along with Henry S. Johnston and John A. Converse, would defend him. His appearance was typical for a boy of his day and age. The broad collar of a light blue shirt lay outside his well-worn brown jacket, set off by a large, red silk tie. As Woode looked around the room impassively, a reporter from *The Denver Times* sized him up.

> His head is apparently well shaped; his forehead high, broad and straight; his blue eyes are deep set and overarched by light-colored, barely perceptible eyebrows. His ears are abnormally large and stuck out from his head like spread sails. His nose is slightly flat, but not ill-shaped. His lips are finely chiseled and his chin well modeled. In stature he is about four feet high and altogether is a fair specimen

John Deweese, a well-known and successful attorney in Denver, defended Anton
Woode in both the boy's trials but also
became something of a surrogate father to
him, comforting him during and after his
trials for second-degree murder.

Dick Kreck collection

of the average school boy one meets on the streets every day.

Every seat in the courtroom was taken, forcing some spectators, mainly women, to sit inside the bar, including the dead man's twin sisters who traveled from Rawlins County, Kansas, to be in attendance. They sat, garbed in black, in the front row of spectators through the entire trial and watched the proceedings closely. Sharing the crowded space were the defendant, reporters, lawyers, curious spectators, and court officials. In one corner sat Woode's mother and father, with whom he huddled, accompanied by Deputy Clark, before Judge Burns called the trial to order. Someone commented that if Judge Burns didn't arrive on time, he might not find a seat. He took his still-vacant place at precisely 10 A.M.

Assistant District Attorney Booth Malone, assigned to prosecute the case, began by reading the charges against Woode. In the stark black and white of officialdom, the case was number 8558, "the People vs. Anton Woode." Though he would pursue a conviction in a professional manner, Malone didn't exhibit much enthusiasm for sending an eleven-year-old boy to the gallows. He would never

Judge David V. Burns, mindful of the tender years of the defendant before him, questioned would-be jurors on their view on the death penalty, and lawyers for the defense were careful to select jury-men (women weren't allowed to serve) who were fathers. Prosecutors were reluctant to seek the death penalty for moral reasons and because they feared the governor would overturn such a verdict.

Courtesy Denver Public Library, Western History Collection, Rose & Hopkins, H-21

ask for a first-degree murder verdict, in part because he felt that Governor John L. Routt, reluctant to see such a young perpetrator hanged, would commute the sentence.

The first order of business, jury selection, was a tedious process. Not surprisingly, Woode found the proceedings boring. As the questioning dragged on, Woode, who took up only a small portion of his chair, rested his foot on a rung of Deweese's, his right elbow resting on the table. He cradled his chin in the palm of his hand and fiddled with his hat lying on the table in front of him. From time to time, he busied himself writing on a notepad with a pencil he had borrowed from Deweese. Sometimes, to get his attorney's attention, he would poke him in the back and ask a question or make a request. "Do you think I have many enemies?" "Ask him if he knew Joe Smith."

The line of questioning from both sides made it clear what their strategies would be. Malone asked if a juror was opposed to the death penalty and would be able to follow the law for a verdict. Deweese countered by asking if a man had children and if his opinion could be changed by testimony. Most potential jurors swore they could be fair and impartial. Some said they were opposed to the death penalty and were dismissed. One man revealed that he knew Anton's father, who, he said, frequently drank in the saloon of the Eureka Hotel, 3801 Market Street, which he owned. Another, Horace Bird, who already had been approved by the prosecutor and the defense, told the court, "I don't want to be sworn in until I know one thing. I don't believe in capital punishment and I want to know if there could be such a thing as having to bring in a verdict in the first degree."

Stunned, Judge Burns asked him if he meant he couldn't vote for a first-degree conviction. "That's what I mean. I won't vote for such a verdict." The prosecutor mulled that turn of events for moment, then, perhaps revealing another bit of his strategy, said, "Oh, well, I won't kick on that. Let it go." Bird was kept on the jury.

Dozens of potential jurors came and went. The interrogations droned on until the lunch break. When court resumed at 2 P.M., Anton Woode's outfit was entirely new—a vested brown suit with knickerbocker pants, black stockings, and lace-up shoes. He sported a blue-and-white striped shirt and a bright blue necktie. A new brown hat completed his ensemble. Where or from whom the new outfit came was a mystery.

The questioning of jurors was not without some humor. F. N. Hassle, the former state librarian, said that he had discussed the murder with his wife and stressed to her the importance of home training for young people. Asked if he had any sons, he replied, "No, sir. My boys have all been girls." The answer caused Woode and others to break into laughter until Judge Burns rapped his gavel to restore order.

Woode sometimes paid close attention to what was going on, but he also grew bored. Shortly after the afternoon session began, he drew a small brown bag of caramels from his coat pocket, spread them on the table, and contemplated which one to chew next. He copied the words "The People vs. Woode" from a large blackboard set up in the court. He even left his chair and crossed the few feet from the defendant's table to sit with his mother and father, his hands in his pants pockets and his new shoes creaking loudly. He whispered in his mother's ear, but she gave no reaction, not even a hint of one.

Completion of the jury took until 5:30 in the afternoon. On the panel (all-male; no women were allowed to serve) were Samuel Higginson, F. J. Harmer, S. A. Bowen, Phineas Graves, Mason Sevy, Eugene Lemmon, John Nelson, Horace Bird, John

Llewellyn, Edward Gallatin, Perry Lovelace, and George D. T. Rouse. All were married and all were fathers. With the jury in place, Judge Burns adjourned until the next day.

DAY TWO, FEBRUARY 28, 1893

Court resumed at 10:15 A.M. Prosecutor Booth Malone stood before the jury and once again explained that, like them, he was merely doing his duty for the law. He clearly had no stomach for seeking the maximum punishment—death—for the young defendant. After a brief opening statement, he called his first witness, Alexander Baker, one of Smith's two hunting companions on the day he was killed. But Baker was nowhere to be found, so Malone asked for Harry Wyman, the third hunter, who was located in the hallway by the bailiff after an extensive search.

Wyman had little to add to what was already known: He, Smith, and Baker had set out from Denver early on the morning of November 2 and encountered Woode, who was hunting rabbits. Smith and Woode went off together while Baker and Wyman headed for a nearby lake to hunt ducks. Later, he said, they heard a shot, and, when Smith didn't return, they searched for him without success. The next day, they found him dead.

Ultimately located, Baker took the stand and recounted the trip in precise detail. He told of his conversation with Woode about not owning horses or the wagon or a watch. "You have not got anything, have you?" he recalled the boy saying. He also retold visiting the murder site the next day with deputies Bert Holloway and T. J. Thompson and finding Smith's body sprawled on a hillside. He told of seeing the single hole in the back of Smith's coat when they turned him over and of riding with the coroner as Smith's body was carried back to Denver.

Woode tried to look interested but, like any eleven-year-old, his attention flagged. To pass the time, he scribbled on the notepad sitting in his lap and fiddled with his pencil, bouncing the eraser end up and down, up and down on his knee. He seemed to especially enjoy writing his signature with a large flourish. In a childish hand, he scrawled, "Them wisess" [witnesses] and "Mr. E Baker./Mr. H. Whimen." And he signed off with yet another elaborate "Anton Woode," creating large loops with the "A" and the "W."

There were other witnesses for the prosecution, including a land surveyor who explained, with

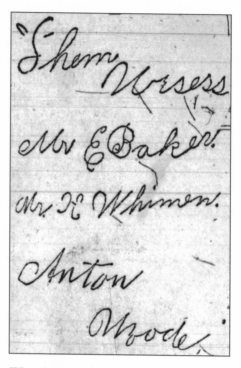

When he grew bored with the proceedings during his first trial in February 1893, Anton Woode passed much of his time at the defendant's table drawing and writing notes. In a child's scrawl he wrote, "Them wisess [witnesses] Mr E Baker Mr H Whimen," approximating the names of prosecution witnesses Alexander Baker and Harry Wyman. He finished the note by signing his name with an elaborate "A" and "W."

a map, where the shooting took place—in Arapahoe (now Denver) County, 400 feet from the Weld County line and seven miles from the Jefferson County line. County Coroner John Chivington took the stand and identified Smith's shotgun and Woode's musket.

There was no way for Anton to know it, but what happened next was a key moment in his trial. Holloway and Thompson, the two deputies who found Woode hiding under his bed and arrested him, each took the stand to explain the boy's first confession to them. Woode's attorney, Deweese, closely questioned both men about their demeanor and conversations with Anton. He was looking for a crack in the prosecution's case, because under Colorado law any confession "induced by promises or threats" was not admissible evidence.

Both deputies denied that they either made promises or threatened the boy as they led him from his house. Thompson did offer, however, that he thought Woode considered him "a friend" and that he held his hand as they walked away from the house. Holloway claimed that Woode "talked freely" and told him that he had wanted Smith's watch. "He had never had anything nice, and he wanted it. He said he didn't want to kill the man but he had to do something to get the watch." Later, Holloway said, he and Assistant District Attorney H. G. Benson visited Woode in the county jail where Woode repeated his confession without coaxing, leading Holloway to conclude that he "knew very well what he was doing."

Deweese objected to the testimony, but Judge Burns let it stand.

Woode's culpability was at the heart of the trial. Did a boy of eleven know evil from good? Would his upbringing leave him vulnerable to wrongdoing? Both attorneys brought experts to the stand. For the prosecution, Dr. J. T. Eskridge testified that he interviewed Woode four days after the shooting and in other meetings. "I concluded that he had enough intelligence to understand the legality or illegality of his acts, and I think he knew the difference between good and evil."

Dr. Eskridge found Woode to be a normal boy. "I went over his career thoroughly, and he shows nothing abnormal for an ordinary boy. His associations and readings, his treatment of the lower animals are all such as I find in the ordinary boy." Further, he testified, the boy was remorseful, another sign that he knew right and wrong. "He cried and said he was very sorry."

As his first witness, Deweese countered with Dr. Eugene Grissom, a specialist in "nervous diseases." It was his opinion that Woode was "emotionally insane," the result of having parents who were plainly of a low order. Woode, he declared, could not be perfectly sound in mind and body. In short, his lack of upbringing left him "an emotional imbecile."

Dr. Grissom unintentionally brought a lighter moment to the proceedings when he responded to Deweese's request to discuss the formation and function of various parts of the brain.

"I could put my finger on the part of the brain if I could have one before me and tell you what you want to know."

"We have no brains here," said Deweese.

"I judged so," said Dr. Grissom.

Once again, Judge Burns was forced to rap soundly for order.

Woode's physical and mental state was a subject of wide discussion, in and out of the courtroom. *The Republican* pronounced him "a freak of nature, in intellect and soul, though not in body." He was, said one observer, "the most innocent being there." The newspaper, reflecting the attitude of many of those crammed into the courtroom, nevertheless declared in no uncertain terms, "Anton Woode is a murderer—

one who has told calmly and, without a tinge of fear or regret, how he stole up behind Joe Smith that day in the field and shot him down." Although the jury had yet to begin deliberations, Woode already was guilty in the pages of the city's newspapers.

Reporters, reflecting a prejudice against immigrants predominant at the time and in sympathy with the boy on trial, viciously attacked his parents in print almost daily. *The Times*'s representative called Woode's mother "just the sort of looking mother to give birth to a child's imperfectly developed mind." When he was first identified as the probable shooter, witnesses called Woode "a Pole," which he was not, having been born either in New York City or in Newark, New Jersey (he claimed both at various times). Authorities and newspapers of the day could not agree on the proper spelling of his first name, variously reported as "Antone," "Anton," and even "Antoine." His mother called him "Toney." Even Woode could not seem to make up his mind; he signed his artwork as Anton, Antoine, or, sometimes, "A. Woode." But on official documents, including the U.S. Census, he was always Anton.

Both his parents, German Russian immigrants who spoke Polish, came to the United States in

1873, then migrated to the Brighton area from New Jersey to labor in the sugar-beet fields when Anton was six months old. Like the Mexican *betabeleros* (beet workers) who followed them into the fields around 1900, these immigrants were regarded as lesser beings, fit only to slave in the spring and the fall in the fields, not to live among the community.

Anton's mother, Maggie, dressed in a ragtag outfit of a green dress overlaid with a red shawl that reflected the family's frugal farm life, took the stand and was lampooned in print. *The Republican* sneered, "The mother is large and all that is unpleasant in appearance. She has heavy jaws, thick lips, high cheek bones, little mean eyes that are stupid more than anything else, and all her features are twisted into a dark, commonplace homeliness that satisfies the eye at one glance." Her husband, Thomas, conceded the reporter, was "less ugly and more malevolent looking."

Born Michelin Drzwilcki, the forty-four-year-old woman said that she had been married twenty-four years and had eight children, but only Anton and an older brother, who died the previous year in reform school at sixteen, survived infancy. At first, she could not recall Anton's birth date, although she ultimately said it was January 15, 1882. While she talked, Woode's father sat nearby, wearing "a long, mud-colored coat and trousers of the same color tucked into his boots." In his brief time on the stand, he was asked, "How many children have you had?"

"None."

"Well, how many has your wife had?"

"Seven and Toney; all the others are dead."

The Republican's reporter sniffed, "They who saw these witnesses on the stand readily understood why Anton was a criminal."

DAY THREE, MARCH 1, 1893

Prosecutor Malone began his closing in a most unusual way. He reiterated that he was given a job and he was doing it. "I enter upon this case as a man and as an officer. I will do my duty and I hope that you, as men and as jurors, will do the same. It is a most remarkable case, this now before us. It is one out of the order of things, for the defendant is a boy—a mere child who has killed a man."

He was sworn to do his duty, he said, and he reiterated Judge Burns's instruction to the jury that it must decide if Anton Woode was guilty of first- or second-degree murder or if he acted on impulse and should be acquitted. There was no other alternative, such as manslaughter, which Woode's attorney had asked for but was denied by the judge. Malone recited the facts of the shooting, then continued to press his case. "The boy committed the murder, and there can be no doubt of it, and I think you will find from the boy's conduct thereafter that his deed was deliberate and cold-blooded. The boy has been cool to a wonderful degree and self-possessed at all times. All things point to him as a cold, calculating little murderer, and we shall ask a verdict of that kind from you." He never uttered Anton's name.

The young defendant showed disinterest. As Malone talked, Woode passed the time by poking his finger into the holes on the back of his attorney's caned chair. Tired of that amusement, he leaned forward and bit the corner of Deweese's chair. Then he rested his chin on its back and stifled a yawn.

After twenty minutes, it was Deweese's turn to make one last appeal to the jury by attacking the prosecution's two principal witnesses, Dr. Eskridge and Deputy Holloway. "I do not consider that there is very much in this case. It seems to me that the court has come to the relief of the jury in assisting them to render a verdict. In the instructions of the court, you see that you are forbidden to find a verdict of guilty in either the first or second degrees of murder unless the people have proven beyond any reasonable doubt that the act was committed with malice and premeditation, and that the slayer of Joseph Smith was capable of judging between right and wrong, and was not a moral imbecile. You will readily see that this has not been done. ... "

Further, he derisively suggested that Dr. Eskridge, whom he scorned as "a paid witness, a patient witness, a witness for money and hire," and Holloway soon would form a partnership to investigate men's sanity, then send them to the state asylum in Pueblo or keep them free, for a price.

Malone was given the final word. Perhaps trying to convince himself that the court's course was the correct one, he said, "Sympathy is a fickle and unreliable thing, but the sentiment of justice is a higher and nobler one. You must not be governed by your feelings. You did not make the law. There are the facts; it is your duty to apply them and to see that society is protected, that the law is obeyed, and let the consequences fall where they may."

He ended his comments by paraphrasing British naval hero Horatio Nelson: "Arapahoe County expects every man on this jury to do his duty."

With a final flourish, he turned toward Woode's parents, with Anton sitting on his mother's lap and holding his father's arm, and said, "Look at that! See what the training of such brutes as those has done for that boy! It has made him the little criminal that he is, and if it had done so, what, in the name of high heaven would follow if such influences were allowed to continue?"

Maggie Woode burst into tears, the first time she had shown emotion during the three days of the trial. Anton threw his arm around his mother's neck and pressed his cheek to hers. Anton's father began to weep quietly. Lacking a handkerchief, he used his coat sleeve. Others in the room were given to tears, too.

At 11:50 A.M., the case was put in the jury's hands.

Chapter Five

Three boys not much older than Anton Woode, book bags slung over their shoulders, loitered among the curious in the crowded hall of the courthouse as the jury deliberations dragged into Thursday, March 2. These were Woode's peers, those whose well-being prosecutor Booth Malone warned about during his closing statement to the jury:

> This case has attracted great public attention, among others that of boys. This boy has been lionized, he has been the cynosure of all eyes. You may say, by your verdict, to the boys of the country, that by taking a gun in their hands and destroying life,

they may become lionized and attract the interest of an entire community, while the law will hold off its hands and let them go unscathed of justice. You may protect society by saying to this boy and other boys watching the case, here and abroad, that Colorado juries will do their duty, and that no mock sentiment will govern them.

Courtroom observers predicted a speedy verdict when court resumed at 10 A.M. Once again, the courtroom was packed, every seat filled and onlookers lined up along the walls. The only four women in attendance were given seats inside the railing. Judge Burns filled the wait for the verdict by dispensing with a civil case. Rumors, later discounted, leaked out that the jury stood eleven to one for conviction. Noon passed, then one o'clock, then two. The jury walked to lunch, protected from the crowds in and out of the courtroom by a cordon of deputies. They spoke to no one, not even to each other, as they left. Still no verdict was forthcoming. Woode and his mother waited all afternoon in the court. From time to time, the boy wandered around the room, even briefly sitting on the laps of bailiff Marsden Sammis and Deputy Tom Clark.

At 2:45 P.M., the jury filed in and foreman Edward Gallatin told Judge Burns that they were unable to agree. The judge was perplexed, and said so. "What is the reason, gentlemen, that you cannot agree? Is it a question of law or of fact upon which you are in doubt?"

"A question of fact, your honor," replied Gallatin.

Judge Burns wasn't prepared to settle for that. "In that case, I think you should take further time for deliberation. The questions submitted to you are only those of fact. You are not to consider the punishment at all. That is for the consideration of the court alone. With the consequences of your verdict you have nothing to do. You may retire."

Three hours later, the jury returned. "You still find yourselves unable to arrive at a verdict?" asked Judge Burns.

"Yes," said Gallatin.

Twenty-nine hours had passed since deliberations began. Judge Burns was in no mood to let it go on any longer.

"Gentlemen, it is a matter of regret that you are unable to agree. There is no probability that in any future trial of this case, the evidence will be any stronger." He said to Henry Johnston, "What has the defendant's counsel to say?" Johnston, believing the no-decision to be a victory for Anton, said he felt that the jury had had ample time for deliberation and might as well be dismissed. Prosecutor Malone was not happy. "It is unfortunate that no verdict has been arrived at, in view of the strong evidence presented, but as this is a matter entirely within the discretion of the court, I have no suggestion to make."

Judge Burns pondered for a few moments, then faced the jury and said, testily, "A later jury which will consider the case will have no lighter task than has fallen to you. You are discharged." He didn't thank them for their time.

Johnston leaned over to his young client and said with resignation, "Well, my boy, you've got to be tried again."

"That's all right," Woode responded, showing no emotion. His face brightened. "I guess you'd better send some pie over to the jail with me."

Later, it was revealed that during its lengthy deliberations, members of the jury barely budged in their opinions. Despite polling every thirty minutes, sixty ballots in all, only one juror, Mason Sevy, changed his mind, and he moved only from first- to second-degree murder. The final eight-to-four verdict broke down this way: For conviction—Gallatin, Sevy, Higginson, Harmer, Graves, Lemmon, Llewellyn, and Lovelace. For acquittal—Bird, Nelson, Bowen, and Rouse.

There followed, a newspaperman observed, "one of those incidents which sometimes occur in the trial of criminal cases, arising from the morbid sympathy of a certain type of women for the criminal." "Sickening sentimentality," the *News* labeled it, more directly. Seconds after the jury's dismissal, two women who attended all four days of the trial rushed from their seats and excitedly shook Anton's hands and hugged and kissed him. He attempted to squirm away from them, his embarrassment obvious to those standing nearby. He might have gone to his mother's lap again, but she and Woode's father weren't in the courtroom. They had gone home to Brighton.

The jury's division was over the question of culpability. Was Woode accountable for his murderous action to have that shiny gold watch? Those who favored acquittal argued that he was not. That he was, in short, "morally insane." The other side maintained that he was bright enough to have full knowledge of the crime. The two sides never came close to bridging the gap.

Two days after the trial ended, Malone, who looked upon his prosecution of the case as his civic responsibility, took the unheard-of step of writing an angry, and lengthy, letter to the *News* in which he replayed the trial, particularly the evidence he presented:

> The evidence was clear and conclusive both of the boy's capacity and of the act. Any juror can without doubt find excuses for voting as he wants to if he tries hard enough. But when Mr. Bird [the juror who said before the trial began that he could not sentence anyone to the death penalty] or any other man says there was no evidence showing that Anton Woode had mental capacity to enable him to know the 'legality of his acts' and to 'distinguish between good and evil' he is simply wrong.

His pen fairly dripping sarcasm, Malone concluded, "I sincerely hope, Mr. Editor, that none of the sensitively conscientious jurors who have delayed if not defeated justice will never have any occasion for practical regret."

Woode, who already had spent more than four

months in jail and celebrated his eleventh birthday in a cell, faced a second trial, only two weeks away.

"Rosy cheeked, fair complexioned and his whitish hair neatly trimmed," observed *The Denver Times*, Woode appeared in Judge Burns's court for retrial on March 20, 1893. The newspapers were no more sympathetic to him than they were in the first trial. Despite its all-American-boy description of the defendant, *The Times* went on to say, "Every page of the boy's record since his confinement here proves him a viciously inclined, conscienceless rogue, a thief apparently by instinct, and altogether a confirmed scamp, without any redeeming attribute." It even accused of him stealing from Mrs. Havens, the kindly police matron assigned to care for him.

As before, Woode was defended by John Deweese and Henry Johnston. Booth Malone was back too, but this time as assistant counsel behind District Attorney Robert W. Steele.

Jury selection was a relatively painless procedure, because most of the potential jurors said they hadn't read much about the case, and even if they had, said Judge Burns, it wouldn't affect their ability to sit on the jury. The twelve men in the box were William Parsons, W. G. Campbell, Albion

Anton Woode was decked out in flamboyant style for his second trial, which began on March 20, 1893, after his first trial ended in a hung jury. The day after he was arrested, before his trials took place, he was branded "The Boy Murderer" in the city's five daily newspapers.

Courtesy Colorado State Archives

Vickery, F. N. Stillwell, John McC. Muir, Michael Anderson, Edward Stoddard, Thomas Halleron, Samuel Large, Charles Blackstone, B. L. Douglas, and Frank Thompson. Woode showed no more interest in the selection process than he did at the first trial, content instead to draw sketches of those in the courtroom.

Woode's second appearance before Judge Burns and "a large audience of scientists, psychologists and metaphysicians," noted *The Times*, would be as much about his coffee habit as his understanding of good and evil.

For openers, the defense dropped two bombshells, neither of which was mentioned in the first trial. First, Dr. F. G. Yocum, an expert in "nervous diseases," revealed that both of Woode's parents suffered from traces of syphilis, which the father had contracted and passed on to the mother several years before Anton's birth. This, he theorized, would affect the boy's mental stability. He also told the court that Woode's parents were both of "low intellectual order."

Second, Alexander Baker, one of the three men who encountered Woode on the hunt near Brighton, admitted under questioning from the defense that the three gave Woode "a swallow" of whiskey, which left him, said the defense, mentally impaired. Baker said later, when he was recalled to the witness box by the prosecution, that Woode consumed barely a spoonful of alcohol and showed no effects from it. He wasn't asked, and he didn't comment on, why three adults would offer whiskey to a ten-year-old boy.

More debilitating to his mental health, said Dr. Yocum, was Anton's diet. He ate five times a day and drank up to twenty cups of coffee. His typical menu:

Breakfast—Two or three eggs, bread, pork, and two to four cups of coffee.

10 A.M.—Bread and two to four cups of coffee.

Lunch—Two or three eggs and two to four cups of coffee.

3 P.M.—Bread and butter and two to four cups of coffee.

Supper—Two or three eggs, two plates of cabbage and pork, and two to four cups of coffee.

The result of this diet, Dr. Yocum explained, was to "degenerate" moral growth. It gave Anton large hands and stomach, poorly developed genital organs, and other physical defects. Worse, coffee taken in such large volume would "retard the moral as well as physical growth." Woode, he concluded, was unable to control his emotions. "Insane people kill without a motive and usually shoot or stab in the back."

Dr. Yocum's theories and conclusions took a beating under cross-examination by Malone. Dr. Yocum admitted that he had previously told the prosecutor the boy could tell right from wrong. Dr. Yocum had also told Malone that until he examined Woode's parents, he was unable to discuss hereditary influences. He still had not examined them. Under severe questioning, Dr. Yocum further admitted that Anton was indifferent and showed no fear of punishment for his crime.

The prosecution brought on its own experts. Dr. J. T. Eskridge, who testified in the first trial that "I think he knew the difference between good and evil," was brought back and said that he examined Woode several times between November 1892 and March 1893 and could find no moral or impulsive insanity. He did not, he said, find any traces of syphilis in Anton's brain or in his physical features. Dr. Eskridge simply scoffed at Dr. Yocum's coffee defense.

Through it all, Woode sat impassively, seemingly unaware that his future hinged on the words being said by the doctors. Nearby sat his mother, clothed, said *The Republican*, "in a dingy shawl, her head enveloped in a white worsted nubia, which she kept on the entire day. Her swarthy, suntanned face was expressionless and vacant. ... "

Anton's age, an issue only touched upon in the first trial, was explored in depth. Hattie Bennett, the schoolteacher who taught Woode for the five months he attended school in 1890 and 1891, testified that Anton told her that he would be ten in the fall of 1890. E. P. Smith, a school board member who conducted a school census in 1890, said he interviewed Anton's father, who told him that his son was "between eleven and twelve years old" that year, making him thirteen or fourteen at the time of the shooting and old enough to be sentenced to prison or hanged.

Called to the stand a second time, Woode's mother said that Anton was her fifth-born child. The first, she said, died at eight months; the second at two and a half; Johnny at sixteen in the reformatory in Golden; the fourth just after birth; and the sixth, seventh, and eighth all were born dead.

That matter unresolved, the medical arguments, pro and con, continued late into the night. In closing, Malone disputed the notion that Woode was not mentally and morally responsible for his act, calling it "bosh." Steele, the lead prosecutor, chimed in and ridiculed the idea that too much coffee, pork, and sauerkraut addled Woode's brain. "I have seen in the history of Colorado when a meal such as that would have been fit to set before a president of the United States, and he would have considered it the best meal he had had for a week. If pork and sauerkraut produce insanity, pity the condition of the inhabitants of the German empire." Do not, he appealed to the jury, "let the boy run wild, to kill any human being who happened to possess anything he desired to obtain."

At 9:45 P.M., both sides rested. Judge Burns announced that court would remain in session for thirty minutes to allow the jury time to reach a verdict. It didn't happen, and Judge Burns sent everyone home for the night.

The next morning, after a good night's rest, the jury resumed deliberating, then filed into the box at 9:45 A.M. to announce that they had reached a verdict. Anton nervously drummed his fingers on the defense table, tapped his feet on the floor, and listened for the reading of the verdict. Foreman Anderson passed a small roll of papers to Judge

Burns, who read them deliberately, then said, "Gentlemen, is this your verdict?" All nodded in agreement. Judge Burns handed it to his clerk, Fred Butler, who read, "In the case of the People vs. Anton Woode, we, the jury, find the defendant guilty of murder in the second degree."

Woode didn't understand. He leaned over and asked Deweese what it meant. When the attorney explained it to him, Woode turned pale, flushed slightly, and began to weep into his red silk handkerchief. It was the first time in two trials that he had broken down. "Don't cry about it, Anton," Deweese said gently. But the boy couldn't stop sobbing. Woode and Deweese sat together until Deputy Sheriff William McKissick led Anton away, back to jail where he would await sentencing. Neither of his parents was in the courtroom.

On April 5, 1893, Anton was called back to court for the last time, to be sentenced. Unlike the days during the trial, when crowds jammed the courtroom, only a few spectators, including Anton's mother and father, were in attendance.

Last-minute appeals by Woode's lawyers that the court erred in its instructions to the jury, that witnesses were not asked whether they thought Anton was aware of what he was doing when he pulled the trigger, and that Woode was probably under the influence of alcohol given to him by the three hunters on the day of the murder were brushed aside.

Before he pronounced sentence, Judge Burns again asked Anton's parents his age. They swore that he was only ten when he committed the crime and produced a family Bible with his birth date, January 15, 1882, to prove it. His mother swore Anton was eleven "last January." Although she admitted that she had trouble recalling all her children's birth dates, she was certain of Anton's because she wrote it down. Judge Burns wasn't convinced. "I think the evidence establishes that (the) defendant was above the age of twelve when this deed was committed," he said, making him legally eligible for a prison sentence rather than being sent to a reformatory. However, the jury declined to find him guilty of first-degree murder and, thus, ruled out the possibility of the death penalty.

Judge Burns did what the law required him to do but took no pleasure in it. The slight defendant, wearing his new brown suit, his new brown shoes polished, and his attorneys flanking him, stood bravely before the bench and nervously awaited the court's judgment. "Anton, you have been convicted of murder," he began. "Have you anything to say why judgment should not be pronounced upon you?" Under the best of circumstances, no child would be able to come up with a response. Anton merely looked back at Judge Burns and said, "No, sir," then used his sleeve to sweep away the tears starting to trickle down his cheeks.

Undeterred, the judge continued to lecture him. "The jury has been lenient with you. I hope you will become a better boy in the future. You are a little fellow yet. You can reform if you will and grow up to be an upright man. You have one reprehensible trait. It is that which leads you to steal. You must try to overcome it. If you are a good boy, it may be that something will be done for you hereafter."

His warnings complete, he sentenced Woode to twenty-five years of hard labor in the state penitentiary. His parents broke into copious tears, but the boy showed little emotion. Three days later, Anton Woode, now a convicted murderer, took his first train ride, to Cañon City and to the penitentiary as the youngest prisoner ever incarcerated there.

6 Chapter Six

An imposing sight greeted Anton Woode's young eyes when he made the short trip from the Cañon City train station out Main Street to the Colorado State Penitentiary.

The prison is straight out of a Hollywood set director's imagination. Twenty-foot-high, four-foot-thick stone walls, quarried and built by the inmates themselves, loom over the western edge of the town 125 miles south of Denver. Towers, complete with armed guards, mark the corners of the prison, where even today some 800 medium-security prisoners are incarcerated. Behind the prison rises an escarpment of lime and sandstone, which, until the early part of the twentieth century, provided prisoners with

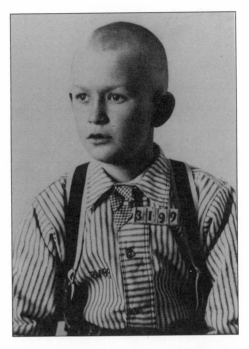

The number "3199" pinned to his chest, a
baby-faced Anton Woode was frisked, disrobed, sprayed for bugs, given a uniform and
bedding, fingerprinted, and photographed
when he entered the Colorado State Penitentiary in Cañon City, Colorado, on April 8,
1893, to begin a twenty-five-year sentence. He
was just eleven years old, making him the
youngest inmate in the prison's history.

Courtesy Museum of Colorado Prisons

hours of labor.

When he entered his new world, known officially today as the Colorado Territorial Correctional Facility and unofficially as "Old Max," Woode, like every prisoner, was frisked, disrobed, sprayed for bugs, given a uniform and bedding, fingerprinted, and photographed. Except for his extremely young age, he was no different from any of the other 513 convicted criminals at the penitentiary in 1893–94.

His "entrance" mug shot, preserved with thousands of others at the Museum of Colorado Prisons, was taken the day he arrived from Denver, April 8, 1893, to begin serving a twenty-five-year sentence of hard labor. It shows a small boy with his head shaved, wearing a striped shirt, a checkered necktie, suspenders, and the number "3199"— by which he would be known for the remainder of his stay— pinned to his shirt. Though he was treated gently by the prison staff, and in many ways was watched over by a succession of wardens, particularly Clarence P. Hoyt and John Cleghorn, Woode was assigned a standard six-by-eight-foot steel cell in the general prison population, although when he first entered the prison he was given a cell to himself. His steel home was Cell House Three, a two-story stone building that ran perpendicular to a central building in the center of the prison where the prisoners' dining room, kitchens, barbershop, guards' dining room, and the warden's office were located.

The prison had been proposed by the territorial legislature in 1868, leading to a spirited competition among several locations, including Golden, Boulder, Denver, and Georgetown, to have it built in their town. Advocates saw it as an economic boon, both in terms of employment and for local suppliers of goods and services. Ultimately, a three-person commission decided that the prison would be built "not more than one-half mile from the business center of Canyon [*sic*] City" on twenty-five acres of land. The first plot was donated by local resident Anson Rudd but was rejected because the land was too close to the center of town and because Rudd was a member of the commission. Though his land was turned down, Rudd served six months as warden at the prison in 1874.

Cañon City's proximity to stone, timber, and iron—all necessary for building the facility—was a factor in the prison being located there, but there was more behind-the-scenes activity, too. Thomas Macon, a Cañon City lawyer and legislator, worked diligently in the General Assembly to deliver the prize by trading votes with those intent on putting

The Colorado State Penitentiary in Cañon City, shown here in 1901, is known today as the Colorado Territorial Correctional Facility, home to 800 medium-security inmates. It is an imposing structure surrounded by twenty-foot-high, four-foot-thick walls built by inmates from stone quarried behind the prison. Anton Woode was put in a standard six-by-eight-foot cell in Cell House Three, where he would spend the next twelve years.

Courtesy Denver Public Library, Western History Collection, X-7815

the new state capital in Denver instead of Golden. Both groups got what they wanted.

After the Rudd property was rejected, Cañon City businessman Jotham Draper donated thirty acres of land located on the west end of town, alongside the road leading to the famous Royal Gorge toward Salida. The extra five acres, he said, were for construction of Soda Springs, a mineral-water spring to be used free by the public. Later, Draper gave an additional ten acres. A number of men, including, once again, Anson Rudd, were nominated for the job of overseeing construction of the new penitentiary, but the position went to local building contractor Samuel N. Hoyt.

By June 1, 1871, the new prison, a single cell house with forty-two one-man cells on two stories, was ready to accept its first inhabitants, but it wasn't until June 13 that the first resident of thousands passed through its iron gates.

When Colorado achieved statehood in 1876, the Colorado Territorial Prison was turned over to the state and renamed the Colorado State Penitentiary. Though it was in many ways an improvement over frontier jails, the Colorado Territorial Prison was considered one of the worst of the Old West prisons. Escapes were frequent, and treatment of prisoners bordered on cruel. When public hangings were abolished in Colorado in 1890, the prison also became the site of forty-five executions by rope.

The penitentiary was built on the model of Auburn Prison in New York state, part of the prison-reform movement of the early nineteenth century. Here, prisoners were kept in an environment designed to teach moral habits of order through severe discipline. Work was good for them. Inmates labored ten hours a day, six days a week. There were no education programs and no job training, ideas that wouldn't take hold until the late 1800s when the National Congress of Prisons outlined more humane treatment of prisoners. Toilets and running water weren't installed in individual CSP cells until 1916.

A major goal was to make prisons economically self-sufficient. In her book *At Hard Labor*, Elinor Myers McGinn wrote, "Historically, incarceration and inmate labor became bedfellows for a variety of reasons. Whether inmate labor served for punishment, for reform or rehabilitation, for profit to the state or to pay the cost of incarceration, for discipline to control certain segments of society, it persisted as the *sine qua non* of imprisonment."

Inmate behavior was strictly controlled at Cañon

City. Prisoners wore striped jackets and pants. A Denver reporter visiting the prison at the turn of the twentieth century made a fashion statement of the uniforms, noting that the men were "attired in white woolen suits which were handsomely decorated with black stripes." These striped uniforms would not be phased out at CSP until 1911. The men were forbidden to talk while eating or working and marched in lockstep with their left hand resting on the shoulder of the man in front of them when walking outside their cells.

A guard who worked at the prison from 1896 until 1899 carefully recorded in a small notebook some of the violations for which prisoners were punished. Among the obvious were fighting, drunkenness, and insolence, but infractions also included throwing stones at other inmates, operating a still, "striking 3409 with a night bucket," "laughing and talking," "singing in his cell," and even "drawing unflattering caricatures of the warden" on a cell wall. Punishments varied from days in solitary to attachment to a seventy-pound ball and chain. There was an ingenious, albeit cruel, form of punishment devised by Warden Hoyt called the "Old Gray Mare" in which a prisoner was forced to bend over a padded sawhorse to be smacked on his backside with a leather strap laced with brass studs and soaked in water.

As an example of a typical punishment, in July 1896, prisoner Frank "Kid" Wallace, a nineteen-year-old who began a seven-year sentence for robbery in September 1895, was reported for "wasting bread." He was given two days in solitary, lost privileges for thirty days, and lost "good time," usually deducted from the end of a prisoner's sentence. Greater punishments lay ahead for him.

Overcrowding was a constant almost from the day the prison received its first inmates. As fast as new cell houses were built, they filled up. Hoyt reported in 1884 that there were 372 prisoners and 312 cells. In 1888, he wrote in his biennial report to the governor, "I am compelled to put more than one prisoner in a cell, and that is not right. It brings in contact those that should be separated, retards discipline and moral development, and is unhealthy." He mentioned in 1900, "The cell houses have been so crowded that it became necessary to put sleeping cots in the corridors. … " There were 514 prisoners but only 444 cells at that time. A third cell house opened in 1900. A separate cell house for women wasn't built until 1895.

As grim as young Anton Woode's surroundings

were, he made good use of his time behind bars. His life at home in Brighton had been far from idyllic. He had drunk alcohol and coffee in copious quantities and attended school only sporadically. In his twelve years behind bars, he worked hard to educate himself, laboring to gain the education that eluded him as a boy. Far younger than his peers, he generally avoided contact with other prisoners, preferring to spend his spare time in the prison library and practice his interest in music and art. Near the end of his sentence, he became conductor of the prison band for a time. He was, in fact, a model prisoner, "quiet and submissive," said one of his wardens.

As strict as discipline inside the walls was, food was not a problem. Hoyt said he "always maintained that a full stomach was a great promoter of good discipline, and that plenty of employment was absolutely necessary." The menu was heavily laden with beef, breakfast, lunch, and dinner. A typical Sunday breakfast consisted of hash, coffee, and vinegar. Sunday dinner was beef, mashed potatoes, gravy, tea, and celery. On holidays, each prisoner was given lemonade, ginger cake, half a pie, fresh pork, and applesauce. Woode thrived on this generous fare. A scrawny boy when he was admitted, he blossomed into adulthood and, by the time he was eighteen, stood five foot ten and a half, although he was a slender 140 pounds.

The penitentiary was frequently a convenient dumping ground for political patronage. Relatives, cronies, and friends were given jobs, often in critical positions as guards, particularly after the economic collapse of 1893 when Colorado jobs were at a premium. Cleghorn, who served two separate terms as warden, complained to Governor James H. Peabody in 1903:

> I have always advocated the enactment of civil service rules governing the employees of state institutions, but more especially those of a penal nature. No sooner is a warden appointed, under existing conditions, than he is besieged with applications for positions from sources more or less political and it must necessarily follow that many positions are filled with men who have no fitness for the duties required of them beyond the fact that they come well recommended.

Some had no qualifications beyond their political backing. Three-time warden Hoyt recalled that during one of his periods as head of the prison, a jobseeker "bearing good letters from a political boss" had only one arm and only one finger on his only hand. The applicant declined the job after being told what it entailed. In 1899, Hoyt wrote to the governor, who was also his friend, that he was being swamped with politically connected applicants. "These outsiders who are asking for these rapid appointments simply know nothing of the condition of affairs here." Among the applicants, he told Governor Charles Thomas, were "an old man crippled up with rheumatism," "a weak sister," one "afflicted with a tumor," "a broken-down soldier," and "an old man, his eyesight partially gone, quite deaf." A guard he fired, he reported, "was absolutely worthless while here with (Warden) Cleghorn. He lost two men from inside the walls while he was on duty."

Nepotism was rampant. In 1892, Frank McLister was named warden, but following the elections, new governor Davis Waite appointed his son-in-law deputy warden. It wasn't long before the new appointee began to complain that McLister had better living conditions, his housing and food supplied by the state. He thought he should have the same deal. A bizarre series of events followed.

McLister, tired of his new assistant's complaining, fired him. In turn, Waite fired McLister and replaced him, but McLister wouldn't stay fired, and, after one day out of office, he reclaimed the job by force.

There were three men with the surname "Hoyt" on the payroll while Clarence Hoyt was warden. When John Cleghorn, a lifelong civil servant who ruled the prison as warden on and off until 1909, succeeded McLister in 1895, he hired his son and nephew. James H. Peabody, a Cañon City banker and mine owner, took over the governor's chair in 1902 and promptly made sure his son landed a job as a guard.

Lack of money for maintenance and improvement of the facility was a constant. In 1876, for example, there were only six guards, two of whom worked at night, to watch over eighty-one prisoners. They were paid $25 a month for working six twelve-hour days a week. The budget for the year was only $7,400, if it hadn't already been spent elsewhere, making it an afterthought in the minds of legislators. This forced wardens, in addition to running the day-to-day operations of the prison, to devise various fund-raising schemes, including selling inmate-grown produce. In 1897, the public was allowed to tour inside the walls for a 25-cent admission. Other attempts to make the prison more self-sufficient included a hog farm and a dairy.

The obvious answer was to put the inmates to work. This idea had the full support of *The Denver Times*, which said, "Idleness drives (prisoners) crazy. We should not allow idleness at state expense when they are sentenced to hard labor. Work is reformation."

Many of the men arrived with skills, including carpentry, blacksmithing, and farming, and were put to work to help with the day-to-day operation of the prison. Because of his youth and small size, Woode, who brought no skills to prison other than his outside occupation, listed as "farmer," was not put to work breaking stones. His inclinations were more artistic. He worked in the prison office and, prison lore has it, he was schooled by a college professor (perhaps his cell mate) who taught him French and German. Woode also learned to play the violin and became a passable painter. Idleness was not a problem.

For the general prison population, chores did nothing to teach trades usable when the prisoners were released. Nor did they do anything to enhance the annual budgets or allow wardens to institute the rehabilitation program reformers advocated. Luckily, management found some of the answers literally in its own backyard. A large hogback outside the prison's north wall was a valuable source of lime, burned and used in smelting, and sandstone, quarried and sold for buildings all over the state. Taken together, the two resources netted two-thirds of the money that came into the prison's coffers in some years.

The tragic confluence of mismanagement, inept personnel, and a shortage of funding came together on the night of January 22, 1900, when one of the penitentiary's most famous breakouts exploded. Anton Woode, who had celebrated his eighteenth birthday only a week earlier, was in the middle of it.

Chapter Seven

The knife, honed to a razor's edge, gleamed in the light. Swiftly, again and again, the homemade six-inch blade plunged into William C. Rooney, the twenty-eight-year-old night captain of the guards. Rooney was grabbed suddenly from behind shortly after 10 P.M. on January 22, 1900, and had no chance to cry out. The first thrust of the knife pierced his heart. He sagged to his hands and knees, moaned softly, and fell on his right side. Death was almost instantaneous.

The murderous escape plot was hatched three weeks earlier by two convicts, Charles Wagoner, number 4580, and Thomas Reynolds, number 3883, who then drew a third man, Frank "Kid" Wallace,

Frank "Kid" Wallace was given an additional twenty-five to forty-five years in prison for his role in the death of guard William Rooney during the 1900 escape. Tired, cold, and hungry, he and Anton Woode surrendered meekly on the Shelf Road between Cañon City and Cripple Creek, Colorado, three days later.

Courtesy Colorado State Archives

number 3855, into their plan. The trio decided to put off the break that night because there was a full moon, but three weeks later, as they sat at dinner, Wagoner said, "Let's get up and go now." Anton Woode tagged along as an afterthought.

As Rooney led the four men back to their night jobs in the boiler room, Reynolds and Wagoner pounced on him from behind. He put up more resistance than they thought he would, and he was mortally wounded in the ensuing struggle. After the stabbing, they moved quickly away from the young guard, blood oozing from him to form an ever-widening crimson pool on the guards' dining room floor. Woode did not join the fatal assault. According to one witness, "Woode stood around and watched ... with a smile upon his lips as if finding pleasure in the shedding of blood."

Moving deliberately, the men called boiler room engineer Zell Humphrey into the dining room, where they seized him and dragged him into the nearby barbershop while Woode tarried in the boiler room. "Scared to death," Wallace later told the warden, Woode had to be called back into the dining room. "I hollowed out to Toney and says, 'If you don't go with us fellows, you are going to get into serious trouble. We are going to get away.'"

Faced with this choice, Woode joined the other three. They bound Humphrey hand and foot while Reynolds waved a knife menacingly close to Humphrey's neck and warned, "Now, lad, damn you, don't you move or I'll kill you." Humphrey later told bystanders, "I laid still, you bet." They also grabbed C. F. Malone, the deputy night captain, and tied him up. Both men later were freed by prisoners Fred Stark and Charles Weidman, members of the night boiler room crew who made no move to escape. After his release, Malone told *The Post*, "I would gladly have given $400 at one time for a revolver. You may think it is a pleasant experience to have a desperate man sit down with you with a dagger between his teeth, demanding firearms, but from the little taste I had of such proceedings last night I beg to differ. I never expect to be so near death again and escape. I really expected to have my throat cut."

Guard James White had a bird's-eye view of the attack from the second tier of Cell House Two. "From my door I could look right into the dining room," White told friends. He saw the attack and heard "three faint moans, sounding to me more like the mewing of a cat than proceeding from human lips." White supposed that Rooney was dead and beyond help, so he sprinted to the west end of the cell house, climbed to a window, and shouted to John Lindley, the guard on Tower Four near the prison's west gate, "It's stuck up!" meaning an escape was in progress. Lindley hit the general alarm button, but also anxiously fired his rifle twice, arousing the prison and townspeople. Fire bells in the town began ringing wildly. Warden Hoyt, wearing a nightshirt and barefoot, ran from his house just outside the walls to the prison gates, periodically firing his pistol into the air. Steam billowed into the frigid January night, casting an eerie pall over the turmoil when the escaping prisoners released hot water from two 100-horsepower boilers into the irrigation ditch that passes through the prison grounds. It was a dreamlike atmosphere.

Their steam dissipated, the boilers and dynamos that supplied electricity to the prison slowly shut down, plunging everything into darkness. Prisoner George Grace, serving time for robbery, crawled up on the boilers to get them running again and opened a valve to set the whistle screaming. This outraged the escapees, who threw a bucket of tallow on the drive belt, once again causing the boilers to quit, dousing the lights and silencing the whistle.

With the entire prison enveloped in darkness, the foursome, who had paused to blacken their faces and hands with soot from the boilers, made their dash for the east wall and freedom. A rope ladder with a hook fashioned from a length of gas pipe was tossed over the parapet. Reynolds and Wagoner used it to scale the twenty-foot wall. Wallace and Woode laid a long length of pipe against the wall, which Wallace climbed successfully, but Woode lost his grip and fell to the ground. He ran to the ladder and, with Wallace's help the last few feet, made it to the top.

By the time Wallace and Woode breached the wall, Wagoner and Reynolds were long gone into the dark. Wallace and Woode headed toward the row of lime kilns behind the prison, paused to get a drink from a spring, then took off up Four Mile Creek toward the mining town of Cripple Creek while Wagoner and Reynolds lit out in the direction of Florence, ten miles southeast of Cañon City. In a manner of minutes, all four vanished into the night.

Their escape was abetted by E. D. Kellogg, the guard on Tower Three that overlooked, a mere fifty feet away, the place where the four breached the wall. He told the warden that he was inside the guardhouse eating his lunch when the break took place and didn't hear the sirens or the commotion that followed. Other guards disagreed, saying that Kellogg "lost his nerve" and lay on the guardhouse floor, frightened that a general escape was under way. Hoyt sacked him the next day.

Fear swept the town, carried swiftly on rumors that a wholesale breakout was in progress. "It was said," noted *The Cañon City Record*, "that the entire penitentiary had broken out and was coming up Main Street in a body. Both men and women were scared beyond reason." Men left a dance to rush home and arm themselves. A five-man posse, aided by three bloodhounds, set out immediately, following a scent in the direction of Cripple Creek.

Hoyt, meantime, wasted no time in issuing "Wanted" posters and a $500 reward (later raised to $1,000, thanks to an additional $500 from Governor Charles Thomas) for the escapees. All except Woode had extensive criminal records. Wagoner was described as "one of a desperate gang of saloon holdups" charged with committing nineteen robberies in Denver. Thirty-four years old, he stood six feet tall but weighed only 140 pounds. In prison since August of 1898 for robbery, assault to rob, burglary, and larceny, his body was laced with scars. The description in his prison record read, "Seven vaccination marks right biceps; six vaccination marks left biceps; large red birthmark back of neck, left side; large scar right side of chin; scar inside left knee; large, smooth scar right shin; two scars between base of right thumb and wrist; scar base right thumb inside; scar on end of left index finger." He had failed in an escape attempt the previous September after getting only a few miles away.

As many scars as Wagoner carried, the thirty-four-year-old Reynolds was a palette of tattoos. Sentenced to seven years in 1895 for a store burglary in Mesa County, he was turned down for parole in October 1899. Six feet tall and weighing 150 pounds, he carried an "India ink anchor base of right thumb; India ink star and two dots base left thumb; two scars left index finger; scar second finger left hand; India ink dot on back left hand; India ink coat of arms left forearm."

The meanest of the bunch was Wallace, who often claimed that his only first name was "Kid" but was known to his fellow prisoners and prison officials by his given name, Frank. Twenty-four years old, he'd already spent five years in the penitentiary for his role in the robbery of a Florence & Cripple Creek train near Victor. It was Wallace, his fellows said, who jumped into the cab of the train and forced

Thirty-four-year-old Charles Wagoner, described as "one of a desperate gang of saloon holdups," eluded capture after the 1900 escape. He was reportedly sighted in towns around Colorado, and some theorized that he froze to death. He was never returned to the penitentiary, and, a year after his escape, there was a $250 reward for him.

Courtesy Colorado State Archives

the engineer to stop. According to the "Wanted" poster, he possessed "sunken eyes, wide apart" and was "sickly looking." He was part of an aborted escape attempt in 1899 and would try again in December 1902, but he was cornered and returned to his cell before leaving the prison grounds.

Woode, who turned eighteen on January 15, was described as having "decided blond" hair. And, of course, mention was made of his most prominent feature—his large ears.

The poster ended with "Arrest and wire C. P. Hoyt, warden, Cañon City, Colo."

Two days after the escape and murder, the sad task of sending young Rooney's body home to Golden, Colorado, in the foothills west of Denver, was undertaken. An autopsy revealed that he had been stabbed seven times, twice in the heart, three times in the kidneys, and once in the side and in the shoulder, evidence of the vicious frenzy of the assault. His death added to an already heartbreaking year for the family. Will's brother, Charles, was killed eleven months earlier in a barroom disagreement in Creede, Colorado. Their father, Alexander, died suddenly in 1888 while driving his wagon into Golden. Will's young wife, May, to whom he'd been married only six months, was accompanied on the

Rio Grande train ride to Golden by Hoyt's wife. The young guard, a star football player at Denver East High School who, everyone agreed, had "a jovial disposition," was buried in the Golden cemetery after services at the Johnson Ranch not far from town. His mother's health was so frail that she was not told of her son's death.

In the rugged canyon country north and west of Cañon City toward Cripple Creek, Wallace and Woode were facing long odds in their escape attempt. Neither was prepared for their getaway. When they were captured on January 25, three days after their escape, they were a sorry sight. Despite the freezing conditions, neither wore a hat and only one had on a coat. For three days they had eaten nothing but a little corn, raw chicken, some uncooked turnips, and a few squash roasted over a campfire.

Tired, hungry, and cold, the pair surrendered meekly to their captors, Charles Canterbury and Will Higgins, who tracked them down between the upper and lower tollgates on the stage road still drivable today as the Shelf Road. Their chance capture was a piece of bad luck for them. Canterbury's boys, ages nine and eleven, spotted the escapees digging turnips from their family's garden and hurried to their house to tell their father. Canterbury and Higgins

Twenty-eight-year-old William Rooney, night captain of the guards, was stabbed seven times, twice in the heart, when Anton Woode and three others escaped. Rooney's death was eventually laid at the feet of Kid Wallace, serving time for a train holdup near Victor, Colorado.

The Denver Republican/Colorado Historical Society, OEH 609 came upon them a short distance off the road, five miles short of Cripple Creek. "I could see the men plainly," Canterbury related to the *Rocky Mountain News*. "One was lying down beside the fire, asleep, and the other had just replenished the fire. Their faces were black and they were without hats. The fellow lying on the ground had no coat. It was bitter cold and I could see the fellows were suffering. It would have been an easy matter to kill them." Instead, Canterbury and Higgins called out to them to surrender, which they happily did. Canterbury asked if they had any guns. "They produced a pocket knife and a silver dollar."

Their captors took Woode and Wallace to the upper tollgate, fed them, and gave them hot coffee, then hired a rig to haul them back to Cañon City. Secreted under straw, quilts, and buffalo robes, the two escapees were guarded closely by Canterbury and Higgins, both with their rifles pointed at their prisoners. Fearful of what awaited him and his partner, Wallace asked the men to douse their lantern before they entered the city and nervously questioned Woode, asking if he thought they would get back to the prison alive. At 5:15 A.M., while the town slept, they were slipped back into the penitentiary.

They fared much better than Thomas Reynolds.

The burglar known as "Slim" was captured by local lawmen in Florence on Friday, four days after the breakout. Reynolds and Wagoner, hungry and cold, rapped on the Cronk family's door and asked for a hat and something to eat. Suspicious, Mrs. Cronk alerted the sheriff, who was in the neighborhood with his deputies to investigate a series of burglaries. They spotted the escapees in an empty lot near the Florence & Cripple Creek Railroad depot and gave chase. Wagoner escaped, but they bagged Reynolds after he got tangled in a barbed-wire fence. He was taken to the city jail, which was quickly surrounded by a crowd of men.

Word of Reynolds's capture was relayed within minutes by telephone and telegraph back to Cañon City, and a crowd of 500 men took to the streets near the prison and the train depot to welcome him home. It was said that a caller from Florence even described the buggy, its two-horse team, and the three guards taking Reynolds back to prison. Fearing his prospects, Reynolds asked when he was captured that he be shot before he could be hanged. Anxious to avoid the mob awaiting them, his captors took a roundabout route when they left Florence and crossed to the south side of the Arkansas River, planning to use the First Street bridge to make a sprint for the south gate of the prison.

Halfway across the bridge, the buggy was surrounded by perhaps a hundred men at 10:45 P.M. Three shots were fired to signal that the escaped man had been taken. In less than ten minutes, he was pulled from the buggy by the mob, a noose thrown over his head, and the rope flung over the crossbar of a light pole at First and Main, in front of the prison. But the mob realized the rope was too short. A second rope appeared, and the two were spliced. "Pull away!" someone shouted, and twenty men yanked Reynolds ten feet into the air, but, at the last moment, he was lowered to the ground and asked if he had anything to say. He declined a chance to pray but said, calmly, "Give me a cigarette and let me smoke."

"You can smoke in hell" was the response. For a second time, "exactly as the town clock struck eleven," reported *The Republican* (probably a bit of journalistic license), he was jerked into eternity. While he dangled, slowly strangling, the crowd hooted and hollered, and someone asked if he would "be good now." His only response was a kick of one leg. Then there was no movement. Satisfied with their work, the crowd dispersed, leaving Reynolds slowly twisting through the night, fully visible to the prisoners across the road as they walked from the cell houses to the dining room for breakfast the next morning. *The Cañon City Record* editorialized a week later, "It is more than probable that a more orderly mob never gathered anywhere in the country." Women and children who hadn't attended the hanging gathered to stare at Reynolds's remains until 7 A.M., when the warden ordered the body cut down, which, said one observer, "fell into the wagon like a log."

Reynolds's death left only Charles Wagoner unaccounted for. The frantic search for him took on comic overtones. Day after day, newspaper headlines promised that his capture was only days, if not hours, away. "Officers Confident of Wagoner's Capture" said the *News* one day and "Wagoner Is Hotly Pursued" the next. "Wagoner May Have Frozen to Death" *The Post* theorized a month after his disappearance. The escapee was spotted, in the span of a few weeks, near Pueblo, in Denver, in the tiny towns of Swallows and Beaver, in Georgetown, on a train, and in the mountains. Despite all the running to and fro by posses and bloodhounds, and various "eyewitness" accounts, there is no historical evidence that Wagoner ever returned to his cell. In his 1900 biennial report to Governor Thomas, written

Thomas "Slim" Reynolds was the probable ringleader of the breakout of four
inmates at the Colorado State Penitentiary on January 22, 1900. He was captured four days later and returned to
Cañon City where he was hanged by "an
orderly crowd" in front of the prison. His
last request was "Give me a cigarette and
let me smoke."

Courtesy Colorado State Archives

a year after the escape, Warden Hoyt noted, ungrammatically, in passing, "Wagoner is still at liberty, for whom a standing reward of $250 is offered."

Why did Woode go along with the other three men in the breakout? It wasn't for ill treatment within the prison walls. He had been accorded special treatment by indulgent wardens, had a clean record, continued his education while incarcerated, and was known by prisoners and guards for "his affable manners." Part of the answer lies in a long interview with Hoyt after Woode's return to the penitentiary. Woode said he was afraid of the three other convicts and claimed that he had attempted to meet with the warden several weeks earlier to get a transfer from the powerhouse to some other job in the prison. During the escape, he said, "Wallace came after me and told me if I made one crooked move he would kill me, and he said that if I would go along with him he would take care of me … and they all said the same." In a separate post-escape interview with the warden, Wallace swore that Woode didn't know about the escape until it began. "He didn't know the plans at all, because some of the boys said if he knew, he would give the whole thing away."

In October 1899, only three months before he

joined the escape, Woode penned a thoughtful if rambling appeal to Governor Thomas. He asked the governor, for the sake of his mother's well-being, that he be released after serving six and a half years of his twenty-five-year sentence. He told the governor, "She is the only Mother I have" and swore that if he were released, "I will do everything in my power to become an honorable man in the future and build up a name for myself." His pleas, and his request for a pardon, fell on deaf ears, perhaps leading him to believe that escape was his only way out.

The original of Woode's letter, an edited version of which appeared in the *News* on January 24, 1900, two days after the breakout, still exists in the files of the Colorado State Archives. Neatly written in an even hand typical of the day, it is rife with spelling, punctuation (particularly random commas), and grammatical errors, if not baldly maudlin sentiment. Here is the unedited text of the original letter, complete with Woode's misspellings and tortured composition:

Almost totally self-taught, Anton Woode had a way with words, which he proved in a beautifully scripted if grammatically flawed three-page letter written in October 1899 to Colorado Governor Charles S. Thomas, pleading for release. On the first page, he wrote, "My Mother paid me a visit last monday, and Gov., the image engraved on my heart, was a poor likeness of her, at her present age." Later, he referred to her as "The only Mother I have." He was turned down for parole by the governor.

CANON CITY, COLO. OCTOBER 2, 1899

Governor C. S. Thomas, Denver, Colo.

Dear Sir:

My Mother paid me a visit last monday, and Gov., the image engraved on my heart, was a poor likeness of her, at her present age, for 6 ½ years have wrought a change, unrecognizeable, even by me. The trials and troubles are to great for her, The once serene blue eye, has changed to a pale gray, the smooth brow, wrinkled, by the trouble she has had, with her only child, who was sent to prison very young. And Gov., that only child stands on the prison records without a report against him, but is the satiety of criminologists and the Boy Murderer of the newspapers, which title I am trying to live out, but which I fear will outlive me, but while the world lives and the papers put forth my bad qualities, I am, practicaly speaking dead (for a crime I commited, and of which I knew not the abnormity) with two thoughts, one to become a man, the other, my Dear parents.

My Mother informed me, that she called at the state House a few days ago, and their some one gave her some promises. she told me to wait a while, before, she would say who it was, but, I can come very near guessing who it was. Gov., I sincerely hope that you will carry out all, or any promises, you have or will make to Mother, because another dissapointment would probably be her death, or start bleeding afresh, the old wounds, and she is the only Mother I have, my greatest hope is that I will be allowed to go home, (a sad home) and make it a dwelling of brightness and happiness before its occupants depart from this world to a brighter one. And I strengthen her appeal, with mine, for the privilege of a parole, which will allow me to go home and make it once more cheerful. After serving $6^{1}/_{2}$ yrs. I have found out that my parents have forgiven me for the crime I commited, when but a child, if you will but stop and give my case a little consideration and that I was under the influence of Liquor, and that I will do everything in my power to become an Honorable man in the future, and build up a name for myself, that will, wash off the stain that is on it now and by hard work and by keeping close to my parents, I think that you will forgive me to, by granting me the privilige of a parole. if you will but grant me that privilege I will give you my word as a young man that I will adhere to the conditions that you impose upon me, so that you need never, feel one small pang of regret for giving me a chance to reedem myself. Gov., I ask you for a parole on behalf of my aged parents, who I hope will see their son a free young man to build his fortune and character, which I promise you, I will have both, Hoping dear Governor that you will listen to my appeal and my Dear parents, whom I hope God will spare,

I remain yours very Respectfully,

(signed) A. Woode.
#3199, Canon City—Colorado

All who witnessed the assault on Rooney agreed that Wallace, but not Woode, had participated in the stabbing, but both were handed severe punishments that included ninety-six days in solitary confinement in dark basement dungeon cells made of stone with a barred steel door over which was welded a steel plate with three or four tiny holes to allow air and light to enter. Prisoners were supplied only a wood plank to sleep on and a bucket for a toilet. During their time in the dank and fetid cells, Woode and Wallace were given two meals of bread and water a day by Hoyt, who nevertheless believed "that the dungeon and starvation are the most cruel of all punishments." Remarkably, it was reported a month after he entered solitary that Woode had gained eight pounds. His skin, which had taken on a bluish cast, cleared up. The prison doctor concluded that Woode's more robust appearance was due to the lack of tobacco and cigarettes, to which he was severely addicted and which were withheld.

In 1938, the long-abandoned isolation cells were discovered during demolition of Cell House One, the first housing unit, built in 1871. They were, reported the *Cañon City Daily Record*, "reached by narrow, steep stairs to ... dungeons that were almost similar to those used in ancient castles." When new construction was undertaken, the dungeons were buried beneath rubble and dirt. Warden Roy Best, not known for his kindnesses toward prisoners, said at the time, "They have no place in a modern prison, and we hope we never have to use them or the dark holes again."

Wallace and Woode were tried for the murder of Rooney in the district court at Buena Vista in January 1901. Woode, once again defended by attorney John Deweese, was discharged by the judge for lack of evidence that he took part in the stabbing. Wallace, on the other hand, was identified by several witnesses as one of three men who killed the night captain. Judge M. S. Bailey gave Wallace twenty-five to forty-five additional years in the state penitentiary, despite the inmate's claims that he "confessed" to Warden Hoyt only to get out of solitary confinement. After his sentencing, Wallace said, "I am not guilty." On the night of the breakout, he had only four months to serve until his release.

By attempting escape, Woode lost any "good time" he accumulated and was required by law to finish out his twenty-five-year sentence, meaning he would not be released until April 8, 1918. "It is safe to say that the boy will spend the remainder of his life in prison," *The Post* forecast. The paper had little doubt that he should be kept behind bars. In a story headlined "The Boy Without a Conscience," which appeared the day after the breakout, *The Post* declared that "the lad was practically devoid of conscience and the moral instinct." Further, it said, "A perfect type of the born criminal or criminal degenerate is Anton Woode. There is no doubt about that."

It would take a miracle to get him out of Cañon City now.

Chapter Eight

In the aftermath of the fatal prison break on January 22, 1900, two long-simmering issues leaped back into the public eye.

First, almost from its opening in 1871, the penitentiary was plagued by political meddling. It seemed that everyone had a son, brother, or uncle who needed a job. Second, the escape renewed the debate over reinstatement of the death penalty in Colorado, voted out by the General Assembly in 1897.

The heat was on Warden Clarence P. Hoyt. Four prisoners had successfully gone over the wall, a guard was dead, and one of his prisoners strung up by a mob. Governor Charles S. Thomas, a friend and supporter of Hoyt's, took the train from Denver

Warden Clarence P. Hoyt was widely criticized for the January 1900 escape that resulted in the death of guard William Rooney. An investigation by Governor Charles S. Thomas, who was also Hoyt's friend, concluded that neither he nor the deputy warden were to blame. Budget shortages and political patronage led to lax oversight of prisoners who worked as trusties.

to Cañon City to assess the situation, though he hastened to add that he was there to check out the prison, not the warden. "I wanted to satisfy myself on the condition of the place." And? "It's in pretty bad shape." He stayed for two days and spent much of that time closeted with Hoyt. At the end of his stay, he told reporters, "I cannot discover that either the warden or the deputy warden is to blame for what has happened. Had their orders been obeyed—and it appears they were not—the affair might have been avoided."

A series of high-profile escapes and questions about his accuracy in keeping the prison's financial records left Hoyt vulnerable. The complaints came mainly from members of the Democratic Party, some of whom lusted after his job and accused him of not being enough of a Democrat. He denied the charges of mismanagement and declared in a letter to Governor Thomas that he was "a strong Democrat." He served as warden for three two-year terms (1882–84, 1886–88, and 1898–1900) under five governors— two Republicans and three Democrats—something no warden, before or after, could claim.

His experience and political connections, however, could not protect him from criticism after the breakout that resulted in the grisly death of night guard William Rooney. Why, many wondered, were convicts working at night in such a critical area of the prison, and under a light guard? Less than two months before the escape, Hoyt, faced with budget and staff shortages, moved guards from the cell house corridors to the outer walls. A former guard told *The Republican*, "It was bad management when he allowed four of the worst criminals in the institution to act as trusties in the engine room. If warden Hoyt had adopted the precedent of former wardens and had a guard armed with shotguns in an adjoining room when the convicts came from the engine room, the deplorable affair could not have happened."

Hoyt steadfastly responded to his critics, and, in truth, many of the problems were not of his making. The facilities were deteriorated from financial neglect, and he was chronically short staffed, meaning he had to employ trusties in jobs that otherwise would have gone to civilians, were there money to pay them. Charles Wagoner, one of the most dangerous men in the prison, was the only plumber among the 544 convicts, forcing boiler room engineer Zell Humphrey to employ him, specifically against Hoyt's warning that none of the four men was to work after a 5 P.M. curfew. Humphrey argued that the boilers were in seriously poor condition and needed repair as quickly as possible, and, because there was no money to pay outside workers, he had no choice but to put prisoners to work.

Worse, Hoyt was burdened with political appointees, many of whom had no experience guarding prisoners and were inept or virtually without skills of any kind. Most men would not take work that depended on political patronage because the job could come to a sudden halt depending on which political party was in power. Some could not read the orders they were expected to obey. It was dangerous and demanding work, done by inexperienced men who were sometimes untrained in using a gun yet were expected to keep track of a dozen or more men. "They are supposed to guard convicts who may have had experience in half a dozen different prisons throughout the country and who are familiar with every trick which convicts employ," the beleaguered warden said during the investigation. Denver detective John Burley told the *Rocky Mountain News*, "For a period of four years I was night captain at the Cañon City penitentiary. My experience has taught me that there are a thousand and one ways in which the convicts can get you if you are not always watching them."

W. S. Jones, another former guard, concurred. In a letter written to the *Cañon City Call*, Jones argued, "You will find working at the CSP good men, but they are often not good prison men. They are better fitted for some other kind of work. There is another class of men at the CSP who are no good there nor at any other kind of work but they have a political pull from some friends or relatives, senator, representative or Governor, and they are sent here with letters demanding that they be given employment at the CSP and (the warden) cannot very well refuse to put them on."

Hoyt was forced repeatedly to accept those who had political clout. "Warden Hoyt has trained the men as best he could, with the circumstances as they were," Clarence L. Stonaker of the state board of charities and correction, which oversaw the prison, told the *News*. "In the course of a year (he) has discharged sixty-five incompetents."

Newspapers all over the state, which paid little attention to woes of the prison and prisoners, suddenly turned crusaders. "The Colorado penitentiary lacks two essential things: money for repairs and maintenance and the exclusion of politics in making up the force," said *The Denver Evening Post* in a long editorial on January 26, 1900, four days after the break. "To employ convicts in the operation of the institution is dangerous ... but what is the management of the institution to do when there are no funds with which to employ help? Party politics are well enough in their way, but they are entirely out of place in the running of such an institution. ... "

The Republican, which frequently pointed out slipshod management at the prison, charged:

> If three men and a boy were able, without aid, to murder the armed official in charge and bind two other employees and hold the institution in control for thirty minutes, finally making their escape with apparent ease, the people of Colorado will want to know the full how and why of it. One thing is certain, however, Mr. Hoyt cannot, in his present trouble, throw the burden of responsibility onto the shoulders of his night substitute [Malone]. It is strange that four of the worst convicts under Warden Hoyt's charge were chosen to (do) night trusty work in the engine rooms.

The small *Denver Eye* saw it as a bigger problem:

It is but another manifestation of the Democratic blight which has fallen upon the city, county and state alike. Like every other institution that has come under control of the Democrats, the penitentiary has been farmed out to party workers. It has become part of the Democratic political machine.

The remedy for a state of affairs which permits such deplorable and criminal occurrences as this ... lies not in the restoration of capital punishment, as some newspapers and one judge of the Arapahoe District Court assert but in the application of civil service rules and the appointment of employees solely on the ground of merit.

Hoyt defended his use of trusties. "Let me tell you. Last summer I had eighty-five trusties and (they) worked outside all the way from three to twelve miles from the penitentiary, and [I] only lost three, not counting Stratton." The last man was a sore point, for Hoyt and for the system. A trusty,

James K. Stratton, escaped on October 10, 1899, from the hose house, a small workshop in the middle of the prison where he also lived. The governor sought an investigation.

To make matters worse, six months after the breakout by Woode and his compatriots, Ed Irving, serving a life sentence, walked out of the prison library to freedom. Hoyt told the prison board, "This was a mysterious case, and I do not know how it was accomplished."

The Stratton affair was even more muddled. Stratton, "a burglar, mail robber and all-around thief," was sent to Cañon City in February 1892 for leading a gang of thieves that made its living robbing mailboxes and stealing cash and checks from envelopes. He was serving a twenty-one-year sentence, but not very well. On September 16, 1893, he fled the prison and wasn't seen again until he was arrested in Chicago a year later and returned to Cañon City.

With the pressure on him, Hoyt was determined to get to the bottom of the January 22, 1900, escapes. He hauled Woode, Wallace, and other prisoners into his office on at least two occasions in the weeks immediately following the getaway. He and Stonaker teamed to question the pair closely. It

Anton Woode had just turned eighteen when he broke out of prison with three hardened convicts in 1900. Warden Clarence P. Hoyt questioned fiercely the two imprisoned survivors, and both agreed that Woode went along as an afterthought. He was caught three days later.

Courtesy Museum of Colorado Prisons

was to little avail; their testimonies were confusing and contradictory. Hoyt, disposed kindly toward Woode, gave him every opportunity to understand that the best thing for him and his chances of getting out before his sentence expired was to tell the truth. "I want you to be sure about this matter; take plenty of time and think it over," he said at the beginning of the first interrogation. "I want you to think well, and tell the absolute truth in the matter" and, he reiterated, "tell the whole thing."

Woode, who was only eighteen and literally grew up behind bars, did just that, to a point. Mainly, he made it clear that he had nothing to do with the stabbing of Rooney and that he lagged behind the other three men during the escape. In fact, he said, he had no intention of busting out. He described the details of the murder, including seeing Wagoner with a bloody knife between his teeth. Reynolds, he said, had both hands on the night captain's throat, meaning he could not have done the stabbing. That left Wallace, the man with whom he was captured near Victor. "I saw him (Wallace) jab the knife into him. I saw him very distinctly (stab the guard) twice while they were standing up, after that they all kind of fell forward on the floor." In a second meeting, he changed his story and said it probably was Wagoner he saw do the stabbing.

For his part, Wallace admitted he was armed with a knife but told Hoyt and Stonaker, "The agreement was to try to overpower Rooney. That was just exactly what we did, but someone [meaning not him] killed him, which I am very sorry of." Hoyt pressed the issue.

"Now, Wallace, don't you think that you helped at some of that cutting?"

"No, sir, I don't think I did."

"You don't say that you did not."

"If I cut that man, sir, it was done by my holding him and his throwing his arm down in his struggles. I do not think I stuck my knife into him at all."

Wallace did, however, exonerate Woode from any direct role in the killing, emphasizing that the boy was unarmed, that he stayed away from the guard, and, in fact, had to be called back into the dining room, where the stabbing took place, from the boiler room.

Where Wallace got his knife became a key point with Hoyt. Wallace said he got it from Woode. Later, he said it came from another convict, whom he declined to name.

"Wallace, will you tell me where you got this knife that night?"

"No, I cannot do it."

"Wallace, you must do it. Now I tell you you had better stick to me. In the last sixty (hours) I have saved your life twice. ... You cannot shield yourself; you cannot shield anyone now in this place. Be a man just for a moment, and tell me who gave it to you."

"Reynolds gave it to me."

In interviews with other prisoners, it became clear that it was Reynolds and Wagoner who dealt the fatal blows. This was convenient for Woode and Wallace, because Reynolds was dead and Wagoner was gone, never to be seen at the prison again.

The affair launched an all-out debate on another issue: the death penalty, stricken from the books by the Colorado General Assembly in 1897. Woode was fortunate that the 1900 escape and murder took place when the death penalty was under attack by religious leaders and politicians in Colorado.

De facto suspension of the death penalty began in 1893 with the election of Governor Davis Waite, a death-penalty foe and a man of many causes ahead of their time, including the graduated income tax, a secret ballot system, direct election of senators, and women's suffrage. His administration was plagued by crises, including the Cripple Creek mining strike in 1893; the collapse of the national economy in 1893 caused, in part, by the repeal of the Sherman Silver Act, which devastated the Colorado mining industry; and the "City Hall War" in Denver in 1894 pitting the state's Populist governor against a corrupt police and fire board.

Prodded by abolitionists, Waite opposed the death penalty, and there were no executions during his two-year term as governor, 1893–95, but there were seven legal hangings under his successor, Governor Albert W. McIntire, in 1895 and 1896. In 1897, legislators made it official—no more executions.

During Colorado's prohibition on state-sponsored executions, the citizenry came to view it as their responsibility to step in where the state wouldn't "to suppress wrongdoing." In the days following Reynolds's lynching in Cañon City by a mob of several hundred citizens, the debate over the necessity of a death penalty flamed anew, led by the state's newspaper editors, pro and con, and prohibitionists. "I do not think it was justifiable," said Governor Thomas in a *News* interview the day after Reynolds was left dangling from a light pole in front of the penitentiary. "Violence is never justifiable."

Warden Hoyt was even more appalled. "It was awful. While I recognize the fact that Reynolds was implicated in one of the most heinous crimes ever committed in the Colorado State prison, yet I can't feel it was just the thing to take him out and string him up without giving him a chance for his life. The thought of a lynching is revolting to me."

The citizenry of Cañon City and elsewhere in Colorado saw it differently. "The lynching of Reynolds ... was a protest against the law by which capital punishment was abolished," said *The Republican* in an editorial. *The Cañon City Record*, in a page-one story headlined "Hanged to a Pole," had no doubts: "The practically universal sentiment was that the fellow got what he deserved. The character of the people of Cañon City and the quiet—we may say humane—manner in which the lynching was conducted goes to show that the work was done by cool heads and sober minds and not by a frenzied mob."

A few spoke out for a permanent ban on execution. At his sermon on Sunday, January 28, Reverend David Utter, president of the Colorado Prisoners' Aid Society, who only days before officiated at the funeral services for guard William Rooney, told his Unity Church congregation, "Colorado ought to set a good example to these partially civilized Southern states where lynching is so common. I count it a true mark of civilization for a community to get out of the habit of killing men in any way, by murder, lynching or legal hanging. The wave of feeling in favor of the death penalty should be put aside. All true progress is away from the habit of killing men." Former state attorney general Eugene Engley called those who favored a return to the death penalty "jackals of ignorance and the hyenas of heredity."

Woode's future, nevertheless, was in severe danger. Given his role in the 1900 escape, *The Republican* wondered, "What can be done with the young criminal Antone Woode, who was already in the penitentiary for murder? He is safe in prison again. Safe is the only word to express his present situation. To him the penitentiary was a city of refuge against the just wrath of an outraged people. He may be imprisoned a few years longer than the term for which he was sentenced, but that will be to him no punishment whatever."

The state's last public hanging took place in Denver on a blistering hot afternoon on July 27, 1886, when as many as 15,000 people—men, women, and children—gathered along the banks of Cherry Creek near where it intersects with today's Cherokee Street to watch the execution of Andrew

Green, an African American convicted of murdering a streetcar driver in an attempted holdup. The circuslike atmosphere surrounding the hanging and Green's lingering death—he took eleven and a half minutes to die—marked the last time a man was executed by the state in public in Colorado.

Four years later, in 1890, hangings were removed to the other side of the stone walls of the Colorado State Penitentiary, where ballyhoo and sideshows would not be permitted, before becoming outlawed in 1897. The Reynolds lynching; the pardoning of convicted killer and cannibal Alfred Packer in 1901, Governor Thomas's last official act; and rising public sentiment convinced legislators to vote for reinstatement of state-sanctioned hangings.

The thirteenth Colorado General Assembly, its members overwhelmingly in favor of the return of capital punishment, wrestled with another issue. Five bills dealing with the death penalty for murder were introduced during the 1901 session, which began on January 2. Some favored a return to "the good old days" of execution by rope. Others campaigned for electrocution, a new method just coming into vogue. Those who argued against electrocution did so for financial, not humanitarian, reasons. Senator Lee A. Tanquary, a Populist who represented

Huerfano and Pueblo Counties, noted, "It will cost $24,000 to put up a plant to kill people with electricity. I was at the penitentiary last Sunday, and the warden showed me a very pretty machine to kill people. If we have to kill them, I want it done with that machine, for it don't cost anything."

Months passed. It was not until May 2, 1901—more than a year after the breakout and murder at Cañon City—that "an act fixing the punishment for murder and prescribing the method of carrying the penalty into effect" was made into law. The final version was based on a bill introduced by Representative Charles E. Stubbs, a Democrat from Denver.

Among the provisions of the new law were that the death penalty applied to "willful, deliberate and premeditated killing; or which is committed in the perpetration or attempt to perpetrate any arson, rape, robbery, mayhem or burglary." Juries were to decide whether a man convicted of first-degree murder would receive life in prison or hanging, which was to take place at the state penitentiary in "a suitable room or place enclosed from public view." No one under eighteen years old could be executed. For their efforts in performing the hanging, the warden would receive $50 and the sheriff from the county where the conviction was obtained would receive $25, plus mileage to the penitentiary.

The last man hanged by the state was Walter Jones, a tramp convicted of murdering another tramp aboard a freight train near Palisade, Colorado. The night before his execution, Jones was visited in his cell by a prison official, who told him that he was the last man to die on the gallows and that the more humane method of lethal gas would be used in the future. Jones replied, "What good does that do me?" Future deaths would have had to be more humane than Jones's. *The Post* grimly reported the day after the hanging, "Walter Jones took the 'high jerk' off the black spot in the death chamber at the state penitentiary Friday night and strangled to death in fourteen minutes. ... "

The first man executed by gas was William Cody Kelley on June 22, 1934. Fifty witnesses, many of them doctors who had come to see the effect of cyanide gas on the human body, watched Kelley die. The last of thirty-two men gassed by the state was Luis Monge on June 2, 1967. Gary Davis became the state's first and, as of 2006, only prisoner put to death by lethal injection, on October 13, 1997.

Time and luck on his side, Woode avoided the death penalty as an underaged defendant in 1893 and, as it came out after a thorough investigation by

Capital punishment was a controversial topic in nineteenth-century Colorado and was banned briefly at the turn of the century. The last man executed by rope was murderer Walter Jones, left, hanged on December 1, 1933. Told the night before his execution that he was to be the last man hanged before the more humane gas chamber was put to use, Jones responded, "What good does that do me?" On June 22, 1934, William Cody Kelley, right, became the first man executed with gas. Thirty-two men were killed by gas at the penitentiary between 1934 and 1967.

Courtesy Colorado State Archives

the state, his role in the 1900 escape and murder of William Rooney proved to be so limited that calls for his execution soon faded.

The now grown-up Woode was still alive to redeem himself.

Chapter Nine

The explosion rocked the thick stone walls, blew glass out of windows, and stopped the office clock in the Colorado State Penitentiary at precisely 8 A.M. on June 22, 1903. In an unexpected way, the blast sounded Anton Woode's opportunity to atone for the aborted escape of 1900.

Six of the most desperate inmates in the CSP conspired to literally blow their way out of the prison. How long they were hatching the plot is anyone's guess, but it was long enough to amass a large stash of nitroglycerin and dynamite, so much explosive that they didn't even use it all during their breakout.

The ringleader was Tom Fallon, alias "Slim"

Bradley, a career criminal and repeat jailbreaker serving fourteen years for a saloon holdup in Denver. The others were Kirch Kuykendall (known as "Filipino Kid" because he served with the First Colorado Volunteers in the Philippines during the Spanish-American War), doing fourteen years for a robbery and shoot-out with police at the Independence Mine in Cripple Creek; James Armstrong, a thief and burglar serving three years; Tom "Red" Fisher, twelve years, assault to kill; Cuaz Cordova, four years, assault to murder; and Robert Cain, life, for killing a rival over a girl in Gunnison County in 1901.

The six men feigned illness before roll call on the morning of June 22. When prison doctor Thomas Palmer, cell house guard Clarence Cleghorn (the warden's nephew), and a hospital steward arrived in Cell House Three to check on them, three of the convicts suddenly brandished homemade knives and ordered the trio to disrobe. After three of the inmates changed into their captives' clothes, all six, leaving the three prison officials behind, followed a meandering route through the washhouse and the dining hall before heading toward the prison's main gate. As they exited the dining hall in the middle of the yard, they unexpectedly came across Mrs. Annie Cleghorn, the warden's wife, who had been visiting the women's facility and was warned by an inmate that the escape was about to occur. Kuykendall and Fallon took Mrs. Cleghorn and dining room steward John Keefe hostage and began walking across the yard.

Anton Woode, unaware that an escape was under way because he was working in the deputy warden's office, nevertheless sensed something was wrong and immediately began ringing the prison bell system to sound the alarm. He continued to do so until Kuykendall burst into the office and threatened to cut his throat. After Kuykendall left to rejoin his fellow escapees, Woode ran to alert guards. Warden Cleghorn and his chief clerk, A. R. Frisbie, were at the Strathmore Hotel in downtown Cañon City at the time of the outbreak but, alerted by a phone call from Woode, rushed back to the prison. Cleghorn immediately ordered guards armed with rifles to take up positions along the prison's south wall, where they could get a bead on the prisoners in the yard. He ordered the men "to scatter and pick off the convicts," taking care not to shoot Mrs. Cleghorn.

Using Dr. Palmer, Keefe, and Mrs. Cleghorn as shields, the prisoners slowly worked their way to the main gates. A defiant Kuykendall shouted up to

John Cleghorn served two separate terms as warden at the penitentiary. Cleghorn watched over Anton Woode and was instrumental in securing his parole after Woode alerted guards to an escape attempt in 1903.

Courtesy Denver Public Library, Western History Collection, X17939

the guards, "I'll never be taken alive! I'll not go back into that damned hole. Shoot and be damned!" The guards, fearful of having one of their shots go astray, held their fire. Now at the inner gate, Kuykendall warned the guards while he held a knife to Mrs. Cleghorn's throat, "When that shot is fired we will kill the warden's wife." Everyone waited.

During the pause, Kuykendall loaded the gate's lock with a rag soaked in nitroglycerin and put a match to it. The explosion tore off the steel lock, and the gate swung open. The procedure was repeated with the outer gate. It was this second blast that stopped the prison clock at 8 A.M. The prisoners rushed through the open gate and onto the street and what seemed to be freedom. One of the guards fired, and Mrs. Cleghorn, believing she had been shot, fainted. The escapees tried to drag and carry her, but finally let her drop to the ground and went their separate ways. Guards followed immediately.

Yardmaster Tom Clark pursued Kuykendall toward the railroad tracks south of the prison and caught up with him at the Cañon City Milling Company's ditch, where Kuykendall threatened him with a vial of nitroglycerin. Clark backed off and ran back to the prison to get a rifle. When he returned, he spotted Kuykendall near the ditch and brought him down with a single shot, then walked up to the prostrate prisoner, shot him in the head, and rolled his body into the water.

Discovered hiding in the weeds near where Kuykendall was gunned down, Fisher surrendered meekly to laundryman J. B. Lantz after the latter fired two shots from his pistol. Said Fisher, "Don't shoot anymore, you might hit me with that thing." Armstrong, wearing the prison doctor's suit and coolly walking up River Street, was apprehended by Will Cleghorn, the warden's son and a guard at the prison. Armstrong, who fled the prison in a panic after the guard opened fire, threw up his hands when confronted by Cleghorn. Realizing his shotgun was unloaded, Cleghorn clubbed the escapee over the head, wounding him seriously. Cordova and Cain commandeered a horse and tried to gallop out of town, but a member of a citizens' posse shot and killed the horse, and both men were taken into custody. Fallon was found hiding under a boxcar 500 yards from the prison. He was the last man captured. The whole escape lasted less than ninety minutes. Other than what the warden described as "wrecked nerves," Mrs. Cleghorn was unharmed. All five of the surviving escapees were given sixty days in solitary confinement in the prison dungeons and fed only bread and water.

The escape by the six remained the prison's worst until October 3, 1929, when a riot claimed the lives of eight guards and six inmates.

Following the 1903 escape, officials launched an investigation into how the explosives were obtained. Fallon and Fisher, whose memories were aided by the "hose" method, a process whereby they were stripped naked, put in a cell, and sprayed with a garden hose until they told what they knew, led investigators to the stash of contraband explosives. Two sticks of dynamite were found suspended by strings in a partition wall of the prison tailor shop, and a Vaseline jar full of nitroglycerin was found in Kuykendall's mattress. A four-ounce jar of nitro was found in Kuykendall's pocket after he was killed. Some believed that Kuykendall manufactured the nitroglycerin in his cell, but there was strong evidence that it and the dynamite were smuggled into the penitentiary by former prisoners who, until Warden Cleghorn put a stop to it, were allowed to visit friends still on the inside. The explosives may also have been inside the prison all the time, because both nitroglycerin and dynamite were used to bust up the rock escarpment behind the prison where prisoners did a good deal of work.

Woode was hailed as a hero for his actions. By coincidence, the prison's board of commissioners was meeting in Cañon City the same day as the escape. Board members Louis King, H. L. White, Thomas Bowen and Warden Cleghorn penned a resolution to Governor James H. Peabody recommending that Woode and another prisoner, Thomas Helster, who warned Mrs. Cleghorn of the impending break, be rewarded with executive clemency for helping to break up the escape. It read, in part, "Had it not been for their efforts and prompt action great injury or death might have resulted to Mrs. Cleghorn and others connected with the institution."

Peabody was less than enthusiastic when the request landed on his desk. "I have always been in favor of seeing Anton remain in prison," he told *The Post.* "I shall not issue a pardon to him on my own responsibility and am not saying either that I will pardon him should the (pardon) board recommend it." On July 3, 1903, the state board of pardons met in Denver to consider fifteen applications for parole as part of an annual Fourth of July holiday tradition. Woode was turned down without explanation.

Chapter Ten

Anton Woode, his family, and many influential friends campaigned without rest for his release from the Colorado State Penitentiary almost from the time of his arrival in April 1893. His mother made frequent visits to the governor's office at the state capitol in Denver in 1899, pleading that her son be allowed to come home to the family farm in Brighton. Woode wrote letters to a succession of governors proclaiming that his youthful indiscretion was nothing more than a terrible accident, the product of an alcohol-induced haze, and that he had, in the intervening years, become a human being fit to live among civilized people.

There were several near misses for a parole or

even a pardon. Had he not gotten mixed up in the murderous escape of 1900, his letter to Governor Charles S. Thomas, written in October 1899, might have freed him. Until the aborted escape, the governor was tilted toward giving the eighteen-year-old the release he doggedly pursued. The failed escape in which a guard was murdered led one observer to write in *The Denver Evening Post*, "That Anton is congenitally cursed there is not a shadow of a doubt." The charge of degeneracy, defined by Webster as "a decline in physical, mental or moral qualities," was one that tainted Woode from his first trial in 1893. In a rambling plea for clemency to Governor James H. Peabody in 1903, Woode blamed the media for perpetuating the image of him as a degenerate criminal, especially after the death of guard William Rooney during the 1900 escape. "I, and my exaggerated deeds, were the subjects out of which was manufactured a killing sensationalism, the picturesqueness of which required that I be painted in the blackest colors. The result of all this has been that the press has succeeded in making my name a synonym for degeneracy."

Early in 1902, Anton's parents petitioned Governor James B. Orman to support a parole for Woode to the board of pardons meeting coming up in June, promising that they would keep the young man at home and lead him to a productive life. Newspapers predicted that although his application would probably be contested, he would ultimately be set free. In the end, his case was not even among the dozens reviewed by the board that summer.

Still, he persevered. The following October, Woode wrote a bylined article for the *Philadelphia North American* that focused on his art and was accompanied by several of his drawings. It was an unabashed sales pitch for his underappreciated artistic ability. "I have had an interest in art since my earliest remembrance but ever since the day that I first picked up a brush I have been dissuaded and discouraged in every possible manner to give up 'the thing as a bad job,'" he wrote. Wholly self-taught, he cited well-known artists who relied on their own skills to make their way, including Sir Joshua Reynolds, Jean Francois Millet, and Edward Poynter. "I am sincere in my art, and will always pride myself upon preserving to the last days of my life that receptivity and that susceptibility to new impressions which are the two chief essentials in the maintenance of aesthetic vitality."

A story accompanying Woode's said that Isadore Horwitz, a noted Chicago portrait painter, had offered to give Woode a course in art once he was freed from his Cañon City cell. Others were less enamored of Woode's skills as an artist, calling the level of his work "of some merit." Another who looked at his drawing concluded that it "is without modeling or perspective." *The Denver Republican*, in a lengthy editorial, went even further. "The fact that Woode can draw a little and has some slight capacity for music has been enlarged upon until it has been made to appear that he is a genius of high rank and one whose talents it was a crime to withhold from the world."

If he learned nothing else in prison, Woode became a clever and eloquent writer, a spinner of high-minded phrases, a skill he used to plead his case with politicians, the prison system, and the newspapers. Riding a wave of support and with his usual literary flourish, Woode penned a long letter to Governor Peabody on February 20, 1903. He was not above outright flattery. "Governor Peabody, you who are wise, you who are just; you who have mastered the opposing evils that drag us down; you who have the power to sift and weigh less happy men, will you not listen to me even as a father would listen to his contrite but despairing son?"

He tried to impress on the governor how much

Anton Woode fancied himself a proficient artist, a skill he taught himself while in prison, while others judged him as merely average. This romanticized self-portrait, probably drawn after his release in 1905, shows him as a dapper young man, his ears far less prominent than in real life.

The Denver Times/Courtesy Colorado Historical Society, OEH, 498 he had changed in his ten years behind bars:

> I know, and surely, you will hold me sound
> in this, that a child's mind is impression-
> able, that it was created to receive impres-
> sions. Oh, Governor Peabody, can you
> not, somewhere in the profound depths of
> your soul, feel that there should be an
> exercise of clemency in behalf of him who
> has outgrown every vestige and taint of
> that ungoverned child of eleven years?
> Today I know the enormity of murder. At
> the age of 11 years, alas, I did not.

Woode enhanced his chance at redemption in 1903 when he helped prevent the wholesale break-out by six of his fellow inmates. It caused a renewal of efforts for his parole. In the weeks after the unsuccessful escape, support for clemency grew. The prison board of commissioners, citing his heroism, recommended to the governor that he be released.

Woode's case attracted the support of a prominent and influential ally, Mrs. Madge Reynolds, the wife of Denver oil executive James B. F. Reynolds and well known in philanthropic and society circles. She campaigned for the poverty stricken, the downtrodden, and those she felt had been mistreated, but her main interest was in children, perhaps because she had none of her own. She took dozens of boys and girls into her modest two-story Victorian cottage at 1209 Logan Street until permanent homes could be found for them. She was on the board of the Denver Orphans' Home and worked with other private charities devoted to the welfare of children.

She and her sister, Mary Smiley (their brother was the noted Denver historian Jerome Smiley), visited Woode in Cañon City early in 1903. She pursued his cause with ardor, as she did with many of those in need of assistance. "I am not a woman who showers bouquets on criminals or who writes sonnets to men's eyes," she told *The Post*. "But I see in Anton Woode the crystallizing of a glorious star. There is a world of genius and power within him and all it needs is developing."

The Post and, by extension, its co-owner, Frederick G. Bonfils, ardently supported her efforts on Woode's behalf and found her personal qualities irresistible. "Her plea is plaintive, her argument amazing, her eloquence effective and her perseverance pervading. With such an attorney the chains of Prometheus might have been stricken off," the

Denver society woman Madge Reynolds, a well-known philanthropist who frequently took orphans into her Denver home, worked tirelessly with the governor and the state parole board to help free Anton Woode. She said of him, "I see in Anton Woode the crystallizing of a glorious star."

The Denver Post/Courtesy Colorado Historical Society, OEH 725 paper gushed. The attention showered on Mrs. Reynolds and her cause by the newspaper and its dapper owner led to rumors that the relationship between the two went beyond the platonic or an interest in a common cause.

It appeared by late June, thanks to the work of his benefactor, that Woode would get not just a parole, but a full pardon. Mrs. Reynolds continued her ardent support. "During the ten years he has been in prison," she told the governor, "he has educated himself better than most of our college boys. He can write the most beautiful letter I ever read in my life."

Governor Peabody visited the prison and was said to be willing to approve whatever steps the board of prison commissioners recommended. Yet, despite a positive recommendation from the prison board, the governor had a change of heart and did not offer executive clemency. The board of pardons formally turned down Woode's request for a pardon on July 3, 1903.

Mrs. Reynolds was "disappointed" in the outcome, but she continued to work on Woode's behalf, and so did the persistent Anton Woode. When his plea came before the board of pardons in 1905, he told its members, according to the board's abbreviated version of his appearance:

> (My) only enjoyment was hunting and (I)
> was accompanied by father. ... In November 1892, was out with my father, who had
> given me a big drink of whiskey, as it was
> a bad, stormy day. A man by the name of
> Baker came up with our party; after taking
> drink all around started out again. I shot the
> man by accident and then took his watch
> and ran as fast as I could. When he went
> home parents thought he was sick from
> his actions. Later the truth was learned.

This was Woode's way of bending the facts. During his two trials in 1893, no mention was made of "a bad, stormy day" nor did either of the surviving members of the hunting party from Denver mention that his father was anywhere to be seen that day.

In a November article in the *Rocky Mountain News*, which appeared near the tenth anniversary of the shooting, Woode had told an even more elaborate story of drinking before and after he met the three hunters on the frozen fields near Brighton. The story was as much an appeal for his release as it was a profile of the young prisoner.

"It was on Saturday, I think, the 5th [it was the second] of November 1892 that father went as usual to Denver. I took advantage of it to drink a good deal of beer. It had been snowing and the desire came upon me to hunt," he told the *News*'s reporter. Unlike Woode's previous retellings of the day of the murder, his father is not on the hunt with him nor is there any mention of a desire to have a gold watch belonging to Joseph Smith, the man Woode gunned down. He claimed that after he and Smith separated from the other two hunters, "He (Smith) remarked, 'It is getting terribly cold.' And he pulled a flask from his pocket and drank some. He bid me take a drink, remarking it would help me keep warm, and between us the flask was entirely emptied of its contents."

It was his drunken condition, Woode alleged, not greed, that led to the "accidental" shooting, a tale totally at odds with what he told sheriffs and others shortly after his arrest in 1892. He couldn't believe he had hit Smith, he told the *News*. He tried to revive the man, during which, he said, "His watch and some other small things fell out of one of his pockets." Woode scooped up the watch and ran home.

He concluded, "I am innocent of murder or

any other crime. I do not now doubt that I killed Mr. Smith but it was either by accident or because (of) my mind being benumbed with liquor that I drank before I left home and on the invitation of the unfortunate man, that I knew not what I did."

Several drawings by Woode accompanied the *News* article. "They will only convey a faint idea of what this wonderful boy has accomplished," said the unnamed writer of the story. "Who can doubt that Governor Peabody will act wisely should he release him? It would be an act of wisdom, of justice and of Christian charity to grant the young man the pardon he so earnestly craves."

It didn't happen. Almost two years would pass before Woode's chance at release was revived. The first hints appeared in several newspapers in May 1905. A *Post* headline promised on May 29 "Boy Murderer May Be Freed." But when the board of pardons met in June, Woode was turned down again, this time by a peculiar combination of circumstances. Governor Jesse F. McDonald refused executive clemency, based largely on the insistence of former warden C. P. Hoyt, who argued that Woode was not rehabilitated. He feared that if Woode were set free, he would attempt to harm Hoyt, who was in charge of the prison during the infamous 1900 escape by Woode and three other prisoners. "You bet I'll keep my 'eyes peeled' as to where Woode is," he told *The Post*. "I don't intend to let him get 'the drop' on me." It would be, he warned, only a matter of time before Woode committed another murder. There was lingering ill feeling between the two. In his 1903 letter to Governor Peabody, Woode wrote, "I ... as a boy of 17 was forced to associate with three of, perhaps, the most dangerous criminals in the prison—forced to that association by a man [Hoyt] who claims to have had a vast experience in prison reform." And it was Hoyt who put Woode and Kid Wallace, his companion in the break, in solitary confinement, on bread and water, for three months.

Nevertheless, by August it appeared that Woode was as good as freed, thanks to the untiring efforts of Madge Reynolds, who badgered members of the state board of pardons, and Judge David V. Burns, who sentenced Woode in 1893 yet wrote the governor to support a parole. Even before the board met, Mrs. Reynolds spoke with Woode by telephone, telling him, "You're free, Anton, you're free. Our prayer of years has been answered by God at last." Woode was skeptical; he had been disappointed too many times. Yet he told her, "If it weren't that you were telling me, Mrs. Reynolds, I wouldn't believe it. But, coming from your lips, I know it's true."

On August 5, the governor and the board of pardons were prepared to let the gate swing open for Woode, but a peculiar thing happened. Not content with convincing the board to release Woode, Mrs. Reynolds asked that the decision be postponed for a month so that she could present even more evidence on Woode's behalf. Judge Burns, whose unhappy task it was to send an eleven-year-old to the penitentiary, pleaded Woode's case. He wrote the board:

Had I been privileged to do so, I should have sentenced him to the reformatory at Buena Vista, but the under the law, I was required to sentence him to a term in the penitentiary. ...

In fixing the period of confinement my purpose was to restrain him until such time as his character should be fully developed, for I am satisfied now, as I was then, that his prison surroundings are better for him than his home life.

A unanimous vote of the five-member board of pardons, made up of Governor Peabody, Ralph W. Smith, Dr. L. Edwin Courtney, Ben W. Ritter, and William D. Peirce, was required to set Woode free. Smith was the most reluctant, fearful that if Woode killed again, the board would be blamed for turning him loose before his sentence, due to expire in 1918, was up. Thanks to Mrs. Reynolds, who bombarded Smith with letters while he was in San Francisco on business, Woode was finally granted parole on September 2, 1905, "upon the earnest solicitation of many friends and prominent citizens, together with the recommendation of the warden [John Cleghorn]," the board noted.

"No one can appreciate what I have had to go through these past four years, the obstacles I have had to contend with—and the reverses and rebuffs I met on every side," Mrs. Reynolds told *The Post*. "But it's all over now, and Woode is a free boy, so it was worth the trouble. Oh, I am happy!"

In a bylined article on page one of *The Denver Times*, Woode, now convinced that his parole was real, said, "Of course, I am grateful for the freedom which will be given to me, and I hardly know in what form to express my gratification at the prospect of liberation after these nine long years."

It did not matter that he actually had been incarcerated for more than twelve years.

Since he walked through the gates into the Colorado State Penitentiary on April 8, 1893, Anton Woode had grown into a man, physically and intellectually. He was no ordinary prisoner, beyond the fact that he was only eleven years old when he entered the penitentiary. During his confinement, he learned to speak fluent French and German, read almost every book in the prison library, became a better-than-average violinist and a competent if not outstanding artist. In the 1900 U.S. Census of prisoners in Cañon City, where others listed their occupations as cook, carpenter, laborer, farmer, or miner, Woode wrote, "musician." It was reported later that he was tutored by a college professor incarcerated about the same time he was, although he never mentioned any such "mentor" in any of the numerous letters and articles he penned.

At noon on Tuesday, September 12, 1905, after twelve years, five months, and four days behind bars, Anton Woode walked out of the penitentiary a free man.

Outfitted in a new suit and vest, his shoes buffed, Anton Woode, right, paroled on September 12, 1905, stands outside the prison with Will Cleghorn, a guard and son of the warden, who would accompany Woode to his new home at the Roycroft colony in East Aurora, New York.

The Denver Post/Courtesy Colorado Historical Society, OEH 725

Chapter Eleven

"Free at last!" Anton Woode exulted to Walter Juan Davis, the famed reporter for *The Denver Post* who was with him the day he was set free in Cañon City.

When they were released, prisoners were given a new suit, black and made locally, $10, and a train ticket for as far as they could travel in Colorado. It didn't take them long to figure out that they could purchase a train ticket for a faraway destination such as Julesburg, in the extreme northeast corner of the state, get off the train in Denver, and turn in the balance of the ticket for cash. Some never left Cañon City, spending their money in saloons and on loose women.

Woode, however, was anxious to get out of

During the twelve years he spent behind bars, Anton Woode grew from a small boy into a man. The last photograph taken of him inside the walls shows a twenty-three-year-old with a firm gaze. When he was released, the last words he shouted to his fellow inmates were "Goodbye, boys! God bless you all!"

Courtesy Colorado State Archives

town and get on with his life, but there was last-minute paperwork to tend to. While he waited, he sat down with a piece of prison stationery, embellished it with a small drawing of an artist's palette, and wrote a long and effusive thank-you letter to Madge Reynolds: "Never shall I be able to recompense you for the great sacrifices and for your time and trouble—a labor of pity which, like the man from Nazareth, is akin to love. I ask you to believe that I shall work untiringly and courageously to be all that you would have me be."

Woode told Davis, "I never felt so glad of anything as the fact that I have not entirely wasted all the years. I would hate to go out into the world as ignorant as I came in." He took a few minutes to visit those he was leaving behind, shook hands with guards, and waved to convicts in the yard. "Goodbye, boys!" he shouted. "God bless you all!"

Warden John Cleghorn, who befriended Woode and helped guide his parole to fruition, met him at the prison gate, shook his hand, and said, "Now, Anton, you are free to go. Goodbye, Anton. Go and make a man of yourself."

"I will, warden."

With that, the gates swung open.

Davis and Woode stood briefly outside the

prison while Anton drank in his new world. "Oh, the trees were never so green, nor the sky so blue, and to think I can go where I please and be out in this beautiful outside as much as I want to."

The midday September air was soft and warm. Woode shed his black suit coat and stood bareheaded in his shirtsleeves as he recalled the days leading up to his release. "I have known it was coming, and have been all prepared to go since I got up early this morning but I couldn't know how good this was going to feel. Oh, how good it feels to be out here and know that this big outdoors is all mine again!"

It was time to go. James C. Peabody, the governor's son who worked as a prison guard, and Will Cleghorn, a guard and son of the warden, who were to escort Woode to New York, and their young charge reached the Denver & Rio Grande Railroad station just east of the penitentiary an hour before the *Atlantic Mail* was due. At 5:12 P.M., the train pulled out of Cañon City for Denver with a happy Anton Woode on board, leaving behind the home he had known for more than half his young life.

The world was his, and yet it wasn't.

Many people were less than confident in Woode's abilities to make his way on the outside. Twelve years had passed. He had lived behind the prison's high stone walls, matured from an eleven-year-old boy whose fellow convicts and prison staff were extended family to a man whose only real skills were passable abilities in music and art and a clever way with words. While he was incarcerated, the Victorian era died; the Silver Crash of 1893 crushed Colorado's economy; the Spanish-American War was won; Horace Tabor, Queen Victoria, and Oliver Wendell Holmes died; Colorado became the second state to institute women's suffrage; the Wright brothers made their historic flight; and President William McKinley was assassinated. The world was not holding its breath for the return of Anton Woode.

He had a lot to prove. Early in 1905, he announced his awakening to what was right in the world, thanks to Maud Ballington Booth, cofounder of the Volunteers of America, a diminutive woman with a powerful and forceful preaching style.

Booth affected many men's lives. She found her calling at New York's Sing Sing Prison. Requested by a prisoner to help his family while he was in the penitentiary, she traveled to Ossining, New York, on May 24, 1896, to lecture to the convicts. She told them, "I do not come here to prevent you from paying the just penalty of your crimes;

take your medicine like men. When you have paid the penalty, I will help you. I will nurse you back to health. I will get you work. Above all, I will trust you. It depends on you whether I keep doing so or not." Out of that experience, she formed the Volunteer Prison League on Christmas Eve 1896 and devoted her life to prison reform and prisoners. Until her death in 1948, she was known as "the little mother of the prisons." The VPL's motto was "Look Up and Hope!" and each man who joined the cause was given a certificate and a small white button with a blue star in the center and the league's motto in red to wear on his lapel.

Born Maud Charlesworth in 1865 to an Anglican priest in Surrey, England, she met the handsome and impassioned Ballington Booth, whose father founded the Salvation Army, at a religious meeting in London in 1886. They were married almost immediately, which so enraged her father that he disinherited her. The young couple moved to America and, in 1896, cofounded God's American Volunteers, which, a short time later, became the Volunteers of America, devoted to its mission "to go wherever it was needed and to do whatever work came to hand."

That Woode would turn to "the little mother"

A tiny but powerful preacher and cofounder of Volunteers of America, Maud Ballington Booth, "the little mother of the prisons," was a potent voice for prison reform. Her appearances at the Colorado State Penitentiary inspired Anton Woode to lead a clean life when he got out. He later went to live at Booth's Hope House in New York City before moving to Newburgh, New York, to pursue a career as a painter.

Courtesy Volunteers of America, Colorado Chapter

was no surprise. He surely became aware of her in November 1901 when she made a brief visit to Cañon City to organize a chapter of the VPL among prisoners. By the time she departed, seventy-six men signed on to the league's precepts, which included "I will accept Jesus Christ as my Lord and Saviour," "I will obey the prison rules," and "On leaving prison I will enter some honest employment and become an upright and helpful member of society."

Woode was so moved by her subsequent appearance at the penitentiary in February 1905 as part of her ongoing program to improve living conditions of those in America's prisons that he felt compelled to write one of his typically flowery letters to Madge Reynolds, who told *The Post* that Woode "literally learned to worship the little mother." Woode wrote to his benefactress:

> Mrs. Maud Ballington Booth favored us with two splendid addresses. In listening to the little mother I witnessed a most remarkable exposition of what I might call the doctrine of the human heart. She has a most powerful and independent mind, emancipated from the influence of all authority and devoted to the search

after truth and the splendid work of uplifting the fallen.

Without doubt she is wrapped up head and soul in her work of reclaiming all men and women who have thus far made a failure of their lives. To cherish in their hearts an appreciation of what life may mean, its opportunities and possibilities of development by good, honest, sincere determination to live an earnest, faithful life.

Booth, who believed there were two strong guides in a man's life, was fond of saying, "The words 'Mother' and 'Home' have a magical effect on the most hardened of men and they must be made to have a deep meaning to the present generation." She attempted to give prisoners both. Her assistance went beyond handing miscreants new rules to live by. After their release, she offered them free shelter at one of the Hope Halls sprinkled around the country, and she found them jobs. There were waiters and cooks, carpenters and farmers, and, what may have attracted the ambitious Anton Woode, artists and musicians.

He would not, however, be joining the little

mother in one of her Hope Halls. Instead, as a critical provision of his release, he was to go to the Roycroft colony in East Aurora, New York, to learn a marketable skill and, it was hoped, to learn the benefits of hard work and a disciplined life. Founded in 1893 by one-time freelance newspaperman Elbert Hubbard, the Roycrofters produced books, furniture, and art during the arts and crafts movement. Once again, Madge Reynolds helped pave the way for Woode by guaranteeing two $50 bonds in case he should fail to report, paying his train fare, and promising Hubbard $5 a week for Woode's room and board while he was apprenticing at the colony, an incentive for Hubbard to take on the convicted murderer.

Woode was at the Roycroft colony in East Aurora only a few days when he expressed dissatisfaction. Living under a new name—he was now "Henry Howard"—he quickly became disenchanted with the living and working conditions. The colony was built on "man's joy in work," but Woode didn't experience the joy. When he left prison, he commented to bystanders, "I don't know just what Mr. Elbert Hubbard will want me to do, but I fancy it will be something in the way of painting or drawing, and my knowledge of music may be of some account." It turned out to be nothing of the sort. By September 19, he was begging Warden Cleghorn, who had to approve any change, that he be allowed to leave. He found his days with Hubbard filled with hard labor, not art, and little remuneration. It was factory work where artisans produced furniture, carpets, andirons, pottery, and picture frames. Drawing and music were not salable skills.

"I am entirely dissatisfied with my location," he wrote six days after he left Cañon City. "There are absolutely no opportunities for me to exercise my muscles, nor my sketching abilities, and positively no opening along commercial or clerical lines."

Having lost half his life to a prison sentence, Woode was a twenty-three-year-old in a hurry. He complained to Cleghorn, "Expert workmen obtain but a mere pittance, just enough to sustain life … apprentices receive nothing in the way of recompense but their meals. Nearly everyone here is expected to produce the best that is in him for love of art and the beautiful, and the management reaps the profit." He wanted out. "I am going to ask you to allow me to change my location," Woode wrote. His plan was to reunite in New York City with Maud Ballington Booth, who, he said, "has ever wanted me to come to her home and she would

secure for me suitable remunerative employment."
A telegram to Colorado Governor Jesse F. McDonald on September 29 was even more to the point. "If possible wire me permit to leave East Aurora. Answer immediately at my expense." The governor replied, at whose expense is unknown, that only the warden and the board of pardons could permit him to move elsewhere.

Newspapers in Colorado reprinted his complaints against the Roycrofters, which set off a firestorm of criticism. Members of the board of pardons were adamant that the "audacious" Woode would not dictate to them where he would live. Some suggested that his attempt to relocate was a violation of his parole and that he should be sent back to Cañon City. Hurt and angry, Mrs. Reynolds was "shocked" when she read Woode's letter in *The Post*. "Anton is not a bad boy, but he is no genius, as he imagines. One of his great faults is his egotism. He thinks he towers above everyone else, when as a matter of fact he is a plain, ordinary boy, who has not had a chance to measure his talents with the world. I feared that his cleverness, with the pencil, for instance, might be turned to some bad use after he secured his release."

The Post, which supported Mrs. Reynolds and

her campaign, now turned against Woode. "Is Woode After an Heiress?" the newspaper asked in a large headline. The reporter mused whether Woode was genuine in his desire to reunite with Mrs. Booth and the VPL, "or does he want to get to the large metropolis (so) that he can tear up the town?" There were rumors that he was "smitten with a girl," possibly an heiress who visited him in the penitentiary the previous spring. Some theorized that he wanted to launch a career as an actor.

Woode seemed genuinely surprised by the reaction to his missive. He was never very good with cause and effect. It was, he argued, written as a private letter to a friend. He wrote an apology, of sorts, to the *Buffalo Inquirer* in New York for the harshness of his words. "However, I will stand for every word I said. So far as I am concerned there is no trade to be learned here that I want to learn. I am a musician and would like to perfect myself in that direction." By October, the heat was on the young parolee. He wrote to Governor McDonald, "Since the publication of my personal letter to Cleghorn, it is not best for me to remain at the Roycroft institution." He also said that he had been offered a job as traveling soap salesman, earning $25 a month plus expenses, if he were released from the Roycrofters. "I believe I am right and wise in asking this favor."

On October 20, he got his wish when Cleghorn approved his move from East Aurora to New York City. "Antone Woode Free to Sell Soap or Peanuts," *The Post* chided in a page-one story. "(He) is now at liberty to sell peanuts, pins, pineapples or soap ... as long as he observes the terms of his parole." Woode vowed, "I'll be a man and make something of myself, and I will not die poor, either." It was another new start for the ambitious ex-convict.

Woode went to live at the Hope Hall in New York City with Maud Ballington Booth and her Volunteer Prison League supporters. He held various jobs, including turns as a waiter and as a bookkeeper for a religious calendar company. He was doing well, well enough that in February 1906 he sent Mrs. Reynolds a check for $50 on a loan she gave him and was upbeat enough that he told her, "I hope to pay you the entire amount—$500—this year."

He didn't linger in New York City long. Driven by his love of art, he was attracted to the beauty of the Hudson Valley, where landscape artists flocked, and he made forays into the region to practice his art. In the spring, he settled in the historic Hudson River town of Newburgh, New York, most famous as the headquarters of General George Washington during the Revolutionary War. Once there, he again started life anew. To begin with, he was now known as Charles Henry Howard. Whether he simply assumed the name or changed it legally is unknown. Still pursuing his artistic dreams, he opened a music studio in Newburgh, where one of his violin students was Mabel Terry, a young woman from the nearby town of Balmville. Only twenty-three, she, too, had an artistic bent. She "is a very nice musician and an extremely fine recitationist and elocutionist," Howard wrote to Warden Cleghorn. Howard spilled the details of his past to Mabel, and she forgave all. After a brief courtship, the young couple was married at 8 P.M. on June 4, 1906, in a ceremony presided over by the Reverend W. F. Compton. The newly minted Charles Howard not only used his new name on the marriage license, his father's name became Thomas Howard. Charles was so excited that he immediately wrote to Cleghorn to tell him the news. "I have the pleasure of informing you that I was married last Monday ... to Mabel Estelle Terry, daughter of Hon. Harvey Terry, at one time one of the Newburgh judges."

Never one to downplay his accomplishments or let facts get in the way of his apparent advancement, Howard was less than honest about his new bride's father, who was, in fact, not a former judge but employed as a gardener on the twenty-four-acre estate of Charles S. Jenkins, president of the Newburgh Savings Bank and one of the town's most prominent citizens. When he first arrived in Newburgh, Howard boarded with the Terrys on the Jenkins estate in Balmville.

Howard's career wasn't blossoming. In 1906, he listed his occupation in the Newburgh city directory as "artist." By the next year, he was a "bookkeeper," a much more certain, though less romantic, career for a newly married man. Now the newlyweds were living in their own rented quarters, not with her father. His time in Newburgh was one of the most stable in Woode/Howard's life. He got married, practiced his skills at music and art, bought a house, held a steady job as a bookkeeper, and was, like his wife, much admired for his church work. In his letter to Cleghorn, he noted that he and the new Mrs. Howard were scheduled to play a benefit concert at the Church of St. Agnes, located across the street from another property owned by Jenkins.

The marriage and his apparent successes in New York renewed hopes for a pardon. When he learned of the wedding, Cleghorn said, "His friends in the city who have believed he would make a good record for himself if given a chance favor an unconditional pardon for him." In its recommendation, the board of pardons noted that he had served on parole for a year without incident and that he should be given his pardon "upon the earnest solicitation of many friends and prominent citizens, together with (the) recommendation of the warden [Cleghorn]." Supported by a letter from Cleghorn in which he said he believed "that he is making an honest effort to lead an upright, useful life" and that "his intentions are sincere," Woode received a "full and unconditional pardon" from Governor McDonald on October 15, 1906. Howard's murderous past under his previous identity was officially forgiven.

In 1908, Madge Reynolds, the woman who devoted much of her time and philanthropy to Woode's freedom, succumbed to ongoing heart disease. The Denver newspapers, particularly *The Post*, grieved for her. Still, there were whispers that the paper's publisher, Frederick G. Bonfils, and the woman with a heart big enough for all were more than mere acquaintances. The genesis of this "affair" can be traced to *Timber Line*, the lively but often embellished history of *The Post* written by Gene Fowler in 1933, some fifteen years after his employment as a reporter and editor at the paper ended. In it, Fowler wrote that lacking "all the intimate facts," a biographer "can come only to the brink of a guess."

Fowler went on to register his guess, a hypothetical picture of a horseback ride the couple took the day before Mrs. Reynolds collapsed at her home, a conversation "relative to their future," and Bonfils's swoon upon learning of her death. It is this version of their relationship that has been handed down from historian to scrivener. It is probably no more factual than Fowler's account, in the same book, of Woode shooting down Joseph Smith or of Woode's subsequent capture, neither of which comes close to the scenarios recounted in newspapers and courtroom testimony at the time the murder occurred. Fowler ends his tale with a highly unlikely, tear-jerking scene of the stricken Bonfils gently placing a red rose on Mrs. Reynolds's coffin at her graveside service. This episode is remarkably similar to one that took place in 1903 at the grave of Fowler's own mother, which he recounted in *A Solo in Tom-Toms*, an autobiography of his boyhood days in Denver. "Charles Devlan [his father] took a red carnation from the spray that had on it no card, which lay among the flowers brought from the church. He stood looking into the half-filled grave."

Reflective of her quiet and often unpublicized efforts for others, Madge's funeral was a simple affair conducted by the Reverend David Utter, an outspoken prison reformer who helped in her efforts to free Woode, at her modest Capitol Hill home with a few friends, her house filled with sprays of violets, her favorite. She lies beneath a plain, four-foot-tall gray granite block in Denver's Fairmount Cemetery, which reads only "Madge Smiley Reynolds/1849–1908/*Memoria in aeternia.*"

Howard continued to live a quiet and obscure life in Newburgh, working as a bookkeeper for the local electric company, giving music lessons, and painting, until 1913 when he disappeared suddenly, only to pop up five years later in Menomonie, Wisconsin. Why he and Mabel moved halfway across the country can only be speculated upon, but it may have had something to do with his mother, whom the young Anton characterized in one of his pleas for a pardon as "the only Mother I have" and to whom he was passionately devoted. His father died in Wisconsin in 1905, leaving his widow virtually penniless. After his move to Wisconsin, Howard resumed his career as a bookkeeper in Menomonie, employed by the Kelly Company and, later, by the

Wisconsin Milling Company.

Swept up in the patriotic fervor of World War I, he registered for the draft on September 12, 1918. It was a period, said James Persico in *11/11/11*, his history of the Great War, when American men were "ennobled by patriotism." Howard was thirty-six years old, well beyond the outlines of the conscription law of 1917, which required all men between the ages of twenty-one and thirty to sign up. Failure to register could result in a year in jail. The armed services were devastated by the flu epidemic raging worldwide that fall, and America was desperate for fighting men. Fifty thousand a week were shipping off to France, leading to the possibility that Howard might be inducted, but he was spared because the war ended in November.

A year later, he was prospering. In 1919, he bought a house valued by the town at $2,500 for tax purposes. Yet, in 1923, he sold the property to his neighbor and left town to move to Minneapolis, where he worked as a bookkeeper and accountant.

The man who as a boy was the object of psychological study, scorn, and publicity died in anonymity on March 8, 1950, of lung cancer, the legacy of a smoking habit begun when he was barely ten years old. He was sixty-eight. His entire funeral notice in the *Minneapolis Tribune* took only five lines of type to sum up his life: "HOWARD—Charles H., 1529 Glenwood Ave., on Wed., age 68. Survived by his wife, Mabel. Services Sat. 1:30 Sundseth Funeral Home. Interment Crystal Lake Cemetery." Mabel, his wife of forty-four years, followed him in death on March 15, 1974, at the age of ninety, three days after suffering a stroke. They are buried side by side at Crystal Lake Cemetery in northwest Minneapolis under standard-issue flat brass plaques with names, dates, and a cross.

As he vowed to Madge Reynolds, Maud Ballington Booth, Warden John Cleghorn, and others who expressed faith in him, Woode pursued a useful life and proved that he was not the "degenerate," "moral dwarf," or "boy without a conscience" that he was portrayed to be in the press. When he was released in 1905, he told Mrs. Reynolds, "As I leave here to do battle in the world and to conquer difficulties among strange people, a stranger myself to what the world may hold for me, I want you to ever remember that my gratitude is unbounded and that you have been the ideal in shaping and molding a career that belongs to today. I ask you to believe that I shall work untiringly and courageously to be all that you would have me be."

When Woode's crime was officially forgiven with his 1906 pardon, his jailer and friend John Cleghorn said, "I feel in my heart that he is going to turn out just as we predicted he would when he was released." His crime and time in prison long passed, Anton Woode died as Charles Howard, a book-keeper, absent the fanfare that haunted his early life, a burden he bore almost sixty years earlier as The Boy Murderer, "which title I am trying to live out, but which I fear will outlive me."

Chapter Twelve

In many ways, society's attitude toward juvenile crime and criminals has come full circle. Incarceration, not rehabilitation, is in vogue, as it was at the turn of the twentieth century. Today's youthful offenders are sometimes more violent than their nineteenth-century predecessors, but the root causes of their crimes are remarkably similar— poverty, drugs and alcohol, abusive home lives, lack of education, and parental neglect.

The late 1800s in America, known to historians as the Progressive Era, were rife with social upheaval. Women's suffrage, attacks on big-business trusts, the end of child labor, and numerous strikes by workers for the eight-hour workday were popular causes. Among the reforms was more humane treatment of juvenile criminals, treating them as children instead of adults.

But when Anton Woode entered Colorado's legal system as a ten-year-old child in 1892, there was no legal procedure for dealing with juvenile criminals. In the eyes of the law, a criminal was a criminal, whatever his age. Change came too late for Woode, but for other young criminals, 1903 marked a completely new attitude about juvenile crime, thanks to the influence of Denver judge Benjamin Barr Lindsey, a diminutive man dubbed "the Bull Mouse" by his friend Theodore Roosevelt.

Ben Lindsey, who stood only five-foot-five, barely more than some of his charges, devoted twenty-seven years of his life to the betterment and protection of young people. Along the way, he fought pitched public battles with crooked politicians, the court system, religious leaders, and just about anyone else who got in the way of his unorthodox methods of redeeming young offenders. His supporters idolized him. His friend and fellow reformer George Creel, a one-time newspaperman, said of him, "Not even Francis of Assisi was more pure of life."

No wayward boy or girl had a more ardent

Denver judge Benjamin Barr Lindsey, one of the first to champion the cause of wayward youngsters, counsels one of his charges. In 1903, Lindsey's never-ending efforts led to the formation of a separate system for juvenile offenders in Colorado. Later court decisions tore down much of the system Lindsey and others built.

Courtesy Colorado Historical Society, F50128

defender or a more loyal friend.

Not content to sit surrounded by his legal books in his chambers and try to convince young criminals to go straight, Lindsey hit the streets. He visited the poolrooms, saloons, and wine rooms on Curtis Street. What he saw shocked him. "Last night on Curtis Street, between Seventeenth and Nineteenth streets, there were fifty boys between the ages of twelve and sixteen years shooting craps in gambling houses, most of them were about fourteen or under. In the same district there are wine rooms with young men and girls going in and out."

Clubs such as The Morgue, Arcade, Cottage Club, Robbery, and Inter-Ocean welcomed all with money in their pockets and dreams of instant wealth in their heads. *The Denver Times* recounted the story of an eighteen-year-old who borrowed a silver dollar to play roulette at The Morgue at 17th and Curtis Streets. "Fickle fortune was not with him. He lost. When his last chip had been raked off the table, the boy turned away with his hands in his pockets and ambled about as if he had lost his last friend." It was, said the reporter, the second time that day he had been in the club when he played away $2. "The young boy ... had a mother and several sisters, all of whom are working daily to live respectably."

A girl too small to see over the edge of the table stretches to place her bet at one of the city's many policy houses in a 1903 illustration from *The Denver Times*. The city's saloons, gambling halls, wine rooms, and houses of prostitution were playgrounds for very young children at the turn of the twentieth century.

Courtesy Colorado Historical Society, OEH 498

Such places, warned Lindsey, "corrupt children and make criminals." If children chose a criminal life, they made the transition from childhood almost overnight, because there were no separate courts for juveniles until 1899. In the eyes of the law, they were adults. A twelve-year-old boy charged with stealing fruit was incarcerated with hard-core criminals locked up for assault, theft, or gambling, or young offenders were sent to reformatories or work camps where they labored in fields or shops for little pay until they turned twenty-one.

In February 1903, Lindsey, to demonstrate lack of concern for children incarcerated in the city's jail, called together a group of citizens to investigate. As he often did, he made sure the newspapers were there to cover it. He was a master at using the newspapers, which he called "my megaphones," to put his case before the public. Governor James H. Peabody, Mayor Robert A. Wright Jr., W. I. Hover, president of the board of supervisors, Charles F. Wilson of the Fire and Police Board, and numerous church leaders gathered in Lindsey's chambers to hear testimony from seven boys who had firsthand knowledge of the evils experienced in the jail. The "depravity" in the cells horrified the panel, but it was left up to the public's imagination to determine what it was they learned, because Lindsey would only say afterward, "The public will have simply to guess that nature of the details of the moral depravity and iniquity to which children are subjected in the jail."

The history of dealing with juvenile criminals in the United States is a checkered one. There had been some attempts to establish refuges for juvenile offenders as early as the 1820s, but the first juvenile court designed to deal with the rehabilitation of underaged violators wasn't formed until 1899 in Illinois. Robert E. Shepherd Jr., in his history of juvenile justice, noted that early in the nineteenth century, children under seven were presumed immune from prosecution because they "lacked moral responsibility." Children between the ages of seven and fourteen were "not criminally responsible." There was no such protection for children over fourteen, who were "deemed responsible for their criminal acts as adults." Between 1880 and 1900, nineteen states (Colorado not among them) executed young men between fourteen and seventeen years old.

Despite the lack of juvenile courts in the nineteenth century, some reformers did seek ways to rehabilitate juveniles without the "contamination of incorrigible adults" in prison. The House of Refuge was established in New York in 1824, the Philadelphia House of Refuge in 1828, and there were houses in eight cities by 1850. They kept young offenders from adult criminals, emphasized rehabilitation, and, most important to mid-nineteenth-century thinking, they were limited to children who, it appeared, could be redeemed by treatment. In many cases, the state took over rearing the child. The New York Society for the Prevention of Cruelty of Children, for example, had the power to remove children from their homes and to arrest those who tried to interfere. In 1890, the NYSPCC ruled over the lives of as many as 15,000 children a year.

In Denver, there were numerous private charities that cared for children, including the Mount Saint Vincent's Orphan Asylum, the Denver Orphan's Home, the Working Boys' Home, and the Saint Clara's Orphan Asylum, all part of a rising belief among social reformers that it was possible to turn young offenders away from a life of crime with early intervention. One of those deeply involved was Mrs. William Byers, the wife of the *Rocky Mountain News*'s founder, who established the Working Boys' Home in 1891 and, in 1903, oversaw construction of a $12,000 facility dedicated to her three deceased grandsons at Broadway and Alameda Avenue for the "care and refinement" of twenty-six orphaned boys.

The nation's first juvenile court was established in Cook County (Chicago), Illinois, in 1899. At that same time, Lindsey already was dealing with juvenile offenders in Denver as public guardian and administrator in the Arapahoe County Court under Judge Robert W. Steele, ironically, the same man who had helped prosecute Woode in his second trial in 1893. It was Steele, later appointed to the Colorado Supreme Court, who instituted Juvenile Field Day, a Saturday session of the court where Lindsey held decidedly informal hearings for young miscreants. Two months before the Illinois court was created, the Colorado General Assembly passed the School Law, mandating compulsory education for children seven to sixteen years old.

Lindsey, appointed a county court judge in 1901, seized upon the law to take it far beyond merely requiring children to attend school. He used it to intervene on behalf of lawbreakers under sixteen, to have them charged with "disorderly conduct" rather than as criminals. Such conduct, under Lindsey's broad net, included burglary, railroad depredations, gambling, persistent runaways, forgery, and "general incorrigibility." Later, he expanded his reach to rescue children found to be living in dangerous or immoral situations. Lindsey began with sympathy for children, maintaining that "our laws against crime were as inapplicable to children as they would be to idiots," as he wrote in his famous autobiographical work, *The Beast*. "I soon realized that not only our laws but our whole system of criminal procedures was wrong. It was based upon fear."

In dozens of speeches he delivered all over the country and in articles in magazines, newspapers, government documents, and in books, Lindsey cited many reasons for young people going astray. He charged, at various times, that poverty and the rampant use of alcohol among parents was the cause. Or that "a boy is generally part of most girls' troubles." He didn't let girls off either. He wrote in *The Denver Post* in 1904, "The girls of Denver are directly responsible for this terrible crime [juvenile delinquency]. They permit young boys on the street to make advances to them without remonstrance, or even reporting the matter to their mothers." There were the landladies of seedy apartments in the city's lower districts who allowed young couples to rent their rooms on a temporary basis. Proprietors of tobacco shops, saloons, poolrooms, houses of prostitution, wine rooms, and gaming houses were responsible. And, most culpable of all were the police who failed to crack down on those proprietors and on the children's neglectful parents, which too frequently led to wayward boys and girls growing into adult criminals.

Lindsey struggled daily to turn this tide. On March 7, 1903, the Colorado General Assembly formally created a separate docket, record, and name for the juvenile court by passing An Act Concerning Delinquent Children, who were defined as:

> any child 16 years of age or under such age who violates any law of this state or any city or village ordinance; or who is incorrigible; or who knowingly associates with thieves, vicious or immoral persons; or who is growing up in idleness or crime, or who knowingly visits or enters a house of ill repute or knowingly patronizes or visits any policy shop or place where any gaming device is, or shall be, operated; or who patronizes or visits any saloon or dram shop where intoxicating liquors are sold;

or who patronizes or visits any public pool room or bucket shop; or who wanders about the streets in the night time without being on any lawful business or occupation; or who habitually wanders about any railroad yards or tracks, or jumps or hooks on to any moving train, or enters any car or engine without lawful authority, or who habitually uses vile, obscene, vulgar, profane or indecent language, or is guilty of immoral conduct in any public place or about any school house.

The law virtually allowed the court to become the child's parent, a process known in legal terms as *parens patriae*. The law did something else: it made the parent or any other adult who led a child astray responsible for the child's behavior, as Lindsey reasoned in a long 1904 article in *The Post*:

Supposing a man sends a boy to the saloon, whether it be the manager of the messenger company, a citizen or parent. The individual who did that thing, as well as the barkeeper or saloonkeeper who let the child have the liquor, has contributed to the delinquency of that child. The child was delinquent by the terms of the delinquent act when it visited or entered the saloon; it would neither have visited nor entered the place if the man or woman had not sent it there. Now, is this [law] not just, and is it not doing more than ever to reach the root of the problem?

He concluded, "It is really astonishing how little care and attention is given by many parents to their children. It is troublesome and tiresome very often for them to do their duty. This [law] awakens them to a realizing sense of their responsibility to the child and if not done voluntarily that it can be enforced by the statute in a most salutary manner." He argued that there is no difference between a twelve-year-old abandoned on the streets and a boy who became a thief through the lack of care or the fault of others. "Every case against a child must be judged more from the standard of the child than from that of a man." He didn't hesitate to sensationalize cases in the newspapers, which were equally eager to sensationalize the children's plight. One case that came before him involved a boy and a stolen wheel (bicycle).

"Tommy, how old are you?"

"Eight years."

"Why did you take the wheel, Tommy?"

"I wanted the money to get some whiskey."

"And, my boy, where did you learn to like whiskey?"

"I dunno."

"Oh, yes, you do."

"I like beer just as good."

"When did you first go to the saloon, Tommy?"

"Mama sent me."

Author Gene Fowler and jazz bandleader Paul Whiteman passed through Lindsey's court during their days growing up in Denver. Fowler's reminiscences in *A Solo in Tom-Toms* of his day in court give insight into how an appearance before Lindsey transpired. Fowler and Whiteman, with some of their friends, were hauled before the little judge for pranks against the city's tramway system: Fowler and his friends for putting an explosive charge on the tracks, Whiteman and his pals for greasing the tracks with butter at East 11th Avenue and Sherman Street. Fowler recounted how their day went:

The door to the judge's "courtroom" opened. An attendant singled out the tramway cases. Those among us who had sinned against the corporation entered the presence of Judge Lindsey.

I saw in him a small man with a large head and large, widely spaced eyes. The eyes were friendly, but they saw inside you. The judge sat on no fear-giving high throne, nor was he robed in a black toga. He greeted us cordially, memorized our names, then invited us to sit as a group beside him at the "conference table." There was no one present to take down notes or record testimony. This remarkable man would hold in confidence anything that we might say to him.

Judge Lindsey listened attentively to the charges made by Officer Sellers and the tramway investigator who was appearing against [Fowler's friends] Paul and Red. "Thank you very much, gentlemen," the judge said to the complainants. "Now you may retire. These boys and I will have a heart-to-heart talk."

After the men had gone, Judge Lindsey turned to Whiteman. "Paul, I'm glad to see you again." He then added significantly, "And I believe I am going to see you more often for the next several weeks."

The judge then gave attention to me and my companions. After hearing our saltpeter-and-sulphur admissions, he delivered a probationary sentence similar to that accorded Paul and Red.

"Judge," I asked with much foreboding, "will you tell my Grandma about this when she gets back from Kansas?"

"Anything that goes on in this room is strictly among us pals," he said. "But you yourself will tell your grandmother all about your own case. And she will understand."

Fowler never forgot Lindsey's kindness. "This man spoke truth to adolescent Americans, and from them received truth. He did not bombard them with the thunderclaps of rhetoric or garb them with the sackcloth of the damned. There was a hill of truth, said the judge. Many roads led to its summit."

That was Lindsey's style. In his 1904 report on

the work of the court, he said, "At the opening of court I generally proceed to deliver a short 'Saturday morning talk.' It is made as spicy and interesting as possible. No effort is made to preach to the boys. I talk to them very much as if I were on them discussing some ordinary boy's troubles."

Lindsey was a prolific writer and lecturer. "I could relate cases of this sort interminably," he wrote in *The Beast*. "I have related them, in newspaper interviews, in magazine articles, and from the public platform. And I find that many people have misunderstood me and have accepted my statements as evidence that I have some hypnotic power over boys and can make them do things contrary to their natures. I cannot. I do nothing that any man or woman cannot do by the same method."

His goal was to keep children out of the adult punishment system. "The purpose (is) to protect children from being stigmatized with conviction as criminals, and in letter and spirit is a constant encouragement to personal work and effort," he wrote in *Charities* magazine in 1903. Lindsey was a big believer in work shaping young boys. "They are too constantly occupied with thoughts of 'having a good time,' and some rather perverted notions of what a good time is." And, he argued, "Too many of our boys thus reach the age of moral and legal responsibility without the slightest conception of work. They are too often more concerned as to how much they earn than as to how well they do their work."

This was a particular sore point with Lindsey, who arrived in Denver as a young man in 1887 and, because of the death of his father, became the head of his family and worked hard to support his mother and three brothers. Lindsey described himself "as mildly inoffensive a small boy as ever left a farm—undersized and weakly, so that at the age of seventeen I commonly passed for twelve." Nevertheless, he went to work, earning $10 a month as an office boy for a real-estate company. He also had a newspaper route in the mornings and labored as a janitor at night. "I had that one ambition—to be a lawyer." Eventually, he apprenticed to a Denver attorney, delivering papers, copying letters, and studying law when he could. All this, and the precarious financial condition of his family, led Lindsey to a pivotal moment. He recounted in *The Beast*:

> After a day that had been more than usually discouraging in the office and an evening of exasperated misery at home, I got a revolver and some cartridges, locked

myself in my room, confronted myself desperately in the mirror, put the muzzle of the loaded pistol to my temple and pulled the trigger.

The hammer snapped sharply on the cartridge; a great wave of horror and revulsion swept over me in a rush of blood to my head, and I dropped the revolver on the floor and threw myself on my bed, sobbing and shuddering. By some miracle the cartridge had not exploded ... I went to back to my life with something of a man's determination to crush the circumstances that had almost crushed me.

It was an experience that made him empathetic to the hardships of children. He knew the pressures that ground on them.

The General Assembly, fueled by pressure from Lindsey and others, expanded the School Law in 1907 to include dependent and neglected children and established a juvenile court separate from the Denver County Court, having jurisdiction "in all criminal cases involving children."

Despite his successes, not everyone was enamored of Lindsey or his juvenile court. The Women's

Protective League heavily criticized the court for its handling of rape cases. The WPL cited eighty-four cases of sexual assault that fell under the jurisdiction of Lindsey's court between March 1909 and April 1913 and noted that only sixteen men were punished; the rest were set free. "Had your daughter or sister been one of these girl victims, been ravished, ruined, become a mother, diseased or recruited for the red-light ranks; or some such girl had in turn wrecked your son, debasing and diseasing him, would you then approve of these juvenile court methods of protecting rapists? Does it punish or deter? It does not."

A WPL flyer seeking public support against the court's tendencies asked, "By what right does the judge of the Juvenile Court violate and abrogate the laws of Colorado against the despoilers of girls? The health and moral welfare of the child is of more importance and value than the freedom of such criminals, or maudlin sympathy for them and their relatives."

Even a group of Lindsey's charges rebelled. A group of thirty boys sent to work in beet fields near Fort Collins in July 1903 were quickly disillusioned by farmwork. Promised that the fields were "a grand place to work" with pure air and glorious sunshine, what they found were twelve-hour work-days for $1 a day and meals that consisted of rye bread, beet top greens, buttermilk, and bacon. They walked off the job, went on strike, and told *The Post*, "We do not have to stay there if we do not want to. It is easy to get away."

Mrs. C. E. Dickinson and other socially prominent women wondered whether taking children away from their families and placing them in reformatories or work camps was the best thing for the children, advocating instead reforming the public schools to better deal with errant children. "The parents of these children should be held responsible; the government is becoming too careless," she told *The Post*. The WPL continued its attack on Lindsey, criticizing his $4,000 a year salary in an era when the Denver Dry Goods department store sold summer dresses for $5.95, a movie cost five cents, and a seven-room house in Park Hill was $5,350. In addition, they pointed out that Lindsey's speaking engagements, at a fee of $150 to $200, kept him away from court business for more than five months in 1913.

Lindsey's stormy career as an advocate for young people and, perhaps more egregious, his attacks on the political corruption he saw in Denver's government and the city's power structure would eventually bring him down. An aborted attempt at the governorship in 1906 was followed by a successful reelection as district court judge in 1908. Along the way, Lindsey and his attacks upon the corrupt power structure of Denver business and political leaders made him bitter enemies.

Eventually disillusioned and tired of fighting the power structure, Lindsey and his wife, Henrietta, and their adopted daughter, Benetta, moved to California late in 1927 after he was forced by political and legal pressures to step down as a judge. Before they left, however, he staged, in one of his grandest public performances, what could be described charitably as legal improvisation: the burning of the records of 5,000 girls and women who had come before him in his days with the juvenile court, in a vacant lot at West 13th Avenue and Umatilla Street. Not coincidentally, newspaper reporters and photographers were present. "I was happy in the knowledge that the secrets of thousands of humans I had helped were safe forever from the public gaze," he said in a biography, *The Good Fight.*

He was elected to the superior court in California, but frustrated and brokenhearted by his failure

In a last act of defiance of his political and judicial rivals, in 1927 Judge Benjamin B. Lindsey burns the records of thousands of girls and young women who appeared in his courtroom, to keep them "safe from the public gaze." Lindsey, an adept user of newspapers, which he called "my mega-phones," made sure reporters and pho-tographers were in attendance at the public burning.

to get back to what he loved most, working with children, Lindsey suffered a heart attack on the bench and died on March 26, 1943, at the age of seventy-three. He is reported to have told his wife on his deathbed, "If I've worn myself out, I've done it for children." Gene Fowler eulogized him in *A Solo in Tom-Toms* three years after he died: "Judge Lindsey, denounced by powerful enemies, never took a step backward from a foe or from his own ideals. The story of the boys' lives he influenced and the good he always did for young Americans never will die."

The fight for juvenile justice did not end with Lindsey's death, of course. Though reliance on the personal magnetism of a judge like Ben Lindsey rankled some lawyers and legislators, the juvenile-court system continued to gain strength without it. Ten states had juvenile-court law in 1910, and by 1915 there were juvenile systems in forty-six states, three territories, and the District of Columbia. Thanks to Lindsey and others like him, every state had a juvenile-court system by 1945.

In the 1950s, juvenile courts gained more and more authority over offenders under the age of eighteen, but the law changed dramatically in 1967 because of a U.S. Supreme Court decision involving a fifteen-year-old from Arizona named Gerald Francis Gault. In 1964, Gault, under probation, made a telephone call to his neighbor, asking her, "Are your cherries ripe today?" and "Do you have big bombers?" A juvenile-court hearing decided that he should be sent to detention for "making an obscene phone call" until he turned twenty-one, a six-year sentence, although an adult similarly charged would have received a mere two months in jail and a $50 fine.

Gault's case wound up before the Supreme Court, which ruled that juvenile offenders, like adult defendants, have the right to notice and counsel, to confront and cross-examine witnesses, to protection against self-incrimination, to receive a transcript of the proceedings, and to appellate review. This decision ran counter to the tradition of *parens patriae*, which began with Lindsey and his informal courtroom decisions to have the state assume responsibility for the care of offenders under the age of seventeen. In its decision, the Supreme Court ruled that juvenile-court proceedings violated the due-process clause of the Fourteenth Amendment to the Constitution. The justices wrote, "Juvenile Court history has again demonstrated that unbridled discretion, however benevolently motivated, is frequently a poor substitute for principle and procedure."

The decision was particularly hard on Judge Philip B. Gilliam, a disciple and friend of Lindsey and linchpin of the Denver Juvenile Court from 1940 until 1973. Gilliam, one of four attorneys in his family, was the only judge of the juvenile court for twenty-five years and instituted numerous programs, including a $1 million expansion of the city's juvenile hall, named for him.

But the Gault decision, and the subsequent passage of the Colorado Children's Code, which formalized courtroom procedures for juveniles, undermined many of the special-treatment programs Gilliam advocated. Faced with his beloved juvenile court becoming a mini criminal court and bothered by ill health, Gilliam retired from the court in 1973 but is still remembered fondly by those involved with the court in the years he led it. He died in 1975.

The distinction between juvenile and adult court proceedings was blurred further by the Juvenile Justice and Delinquency Prevention Act of 1974, amended to provide minimum sentencing standards and allow states to try juveniles as adults for some violent crime and weapons violations.

Punishment, not rehabilitation, became the intent, an idea that was pushed even further by a rise, beginning in the late 1980s, in violent crimes involving juveniles.

Frustrated by the juvenile system's inability to deal with increasingly violent youth, governmental bodies, at the urging of their constituents, decided to "get tough" on crime. More and more cases were diverted to adult courts. In 1980, for example, every state put young offenders through its juvenile-court system. By 1995, only Hawaii treated children under sixteen as juveniles.

In a comprehensive four-part series in February 2006, *The Denver Post* charted changes in the ways in which the state deals with juvenile offenders. For example, Colorado began, in 1991, to impose mandatory life sentences without parole. Since then, forty-five juvenile offenders, some as young as fourteen, have been given such sentences.

The majority of young offenders doing life terms are charged with "felony murder," which allows, noted *The Post*, "prosecutors to hold someone responsible if a person died during the commission of certain crimes—even if there was no intent to kill or that person's actions didn't directly cause the death." Colorado is one of fifteen states that allow prosecutors, not judges, to charge juveniles with adult crimes that could lead to life in prison without parole.

The year 1993 was dubbed the "Summer of Violence" by the media in Colorado, even though statistics showed that the year was no more or less violent than previous ones. But there was a new, random element to the deaths—children caught in cross fires. The ugly attacks and shooting deaths of fourteen students and a teacher at Columbine High School in Littleton in April 1999 further raised the call for stricter laws involving young people and guns. These were not boyhood criminals of long-ago times, stealing bicycles and pulling pranks. Bob Grant, a one-time prosecutor and executive director of the Colorado District Attorneys Council, argued that the juvenile system wasn't equipped to deal with violent offenders. "Those, I'm sorry, are not children," he told the *Rocky Mountain News.* "Those are murderers. Those are the worst of the worst." The cycle of dealing with juvenile offenders, which swung toward rehabilitation early in the twentieth century, turned 180 degrees in the beginning of the twenty-first century.

Paradoxically, violent crime among youthful offenders started to decline in the mid-1990s, and so did the fashion for adult punishments. In 2002, the U.S. Supreme Court banned execution of the mentally retarded. Early in 2005, the court, which had allowed states to impose the death penalty for adults since 1976, ruled in a five-to-four decision that the death penalty for juveniles, those under eighteen, violates the Eighth Amendment ban on cruel and unusual punishment. Justice Anthony Kennedy wrote:

> The age of eighteen is the point where society draws the line for many purposes between childhood and adulthood. It is, we conclude, the age at which the line for death eligibility ought to rest. It is proper that we acknowledge the overwhelming weight of international opinion against the juvenile death penalty, resting in large part on the understanding that the instability and emotional imbalance of young people may often be a fact in the crime.

At the time of the decision, there were seventy-two people on death rows who were under eighteen when they committed their crimes. The 2005 decision followed a trend by the court, which in 1988 outlawed executions for those fifteen or younger when they committed their crimes.

The court's decision on executions didn't affect Colorado juveniles convicted of first-degree murder, because the maximum sentence they can receive is life in prison without parole. But even that is controversial. Human Rights Watch, a New York–based group, complained that the Colorado law is cruel, unfair, and unnecessary. "This issue of sentencing juveniles to life without parole is clearly prohibited by human-rights law, and it's astonishing the United States still practices this when 133 countries around the world don't, and in fact never have," a report from the HRW said.

In 1993, Colorado established the Youthful Offenders System as a rehabilitation program for juveniles. On the downside, funding for such systems was reduced by almost $30 million between 2001 and 2005.

At the same time, California, where many social and popular trends begin, revised its California Youth Authority from a punitive system to one with more therapy and positive reinforcement, "a completely different way of doing business," said an attorney. Since its creation in 1941, the agency moved from a paternalistic approach toward offenders to more prisonlike methods to deal with violent youths, particularly gang members aged fourteen to twenty-five. The Supreme Court's 2005 decision blocking the death penalty for juveniles prompted David Darchuk, a prison officer who retired after being stabbed by an inmate at a youth correction facility, to tell the *Los Angeles Times*, "Who wrote this plan, Walt Disney? We're not talking about bicycle thieves and runaways. These are murderers, car jackers, hard-core criminals. Therapy and coloring Crayons aren't going to help."

Even Ben Lindsey, who spent his adult life campaigning for more sympathetic legal treatment of young people, knew that a separate system would not solve the problem of young offenders. "No system is perfect. If anyone conceives the idea that the juvenile court was created for the purpose of correcting or reforming every disorderly child, they are, of course, mistaken. Jails and criminal courts never did that. There are failures under the juvenile law, but there were more failures under the criminal law."

The tale of Anton Woode—his bizarre trip through the nineteenth-century legal system, his incarceration at a tender age, and his ultimate rehabilitation—resonates more than a century later as much for what it says about modern society as for what it tells us about his crime and young life. Children too young to vote or drive are given life sentences in prison instead of diversion to a more humane system, based on their psychological, emotional, and developmental immaturity, where rehabilitation is still possible. In his wisdom with young people, Judge Lindsey looked both backward and forward when he said, "Our aim is to make an individual boy strong enough in himself and in his own character to avoid the wrong and do the right because it is right and best for him."

Sources

Books

Banner, Stuart. *The Death Penalty: An American History*. Cambridge: Harvard University Press, 2002.

Bell, Ernest A. *Fighting the Traffic in Young Girls*. Chicago: G. S. Ball, 1910.

Brighton Genealogy Society. *Brighton, Colorado, and Surrounding Area 1887–1987*, Vol. 1. Dallas: Curtis Media Group, 1987.

Brumberg, Joan Jacobs. *Kansas Charley: The Story of a 19th-Century Boy Murderer*. New York: Viking, 2003.

Cooper, Courtney Ryley. *Designs in Scarlet*. Boston: Little, Brown, 1939.

Creel, George. *Rebel at Large: Recollections of Fifty Crowded Years*. New York: Putnam, 1947.

Evans, Wainwright, and Ben B. Lindsey. *The Revolt of Modern Youth*. New York: Boni & Liveright, 1925.

———. *The Companionate Marriage*. New York: Boni & Liveright, 1927.

Fowler, Gene. *A Solo in Tom-Toms*. New York: Viking Press, 1946.

———. *Timber Line: A Story of Bonfils and Tammen*. Garden City, N.Y.: Halcyon House, 1943.

Fritz, Percy Stanley. *Colorado: The Centennial State*. New York: Prentice-Hall, 1941.

Goodstein, Phil. *Denver from the Bottom Up. Vol 1: From Sand Creek to Ludlow*. Denver: New Social Publications, 2003.

———. *Denver from the Bottom Up. Vol 2: Robert Speer's Denver 1904–1920*. Denver: New Social Publications, 2004.

Grant, Donald L. *The Anti-Lynching Movement: 1883–1932*. San Francisco: R and E Research Associates, 1975.

Hartman, Diane, and Alan J. Kania. *The Bench and the Bar: A Centennial View of Denver's Legal History*. Denver: Windsor Publications, 1993.

Larsen, Charles. *The Good Fight: The Life and

Times of Ben B. Lindsey. Chicago: Quadrangle, 1972.

Leonard, Stephen J. *Lynching in Colorado 1859–1919.* Boulder: University Press of Colorado, 2002.

Leonard, Stephen J., and Thomas J. Noel. *Denver: Mining Camp to Metropolis.* Boulder, Colorado: University Press of Colorado, 1990.

McGinn, Elinor Myers. *At Hard Labor: Inmate Labor at the Colorado State Penitentiary, 1871–1940.* New York: Peter Lang, 1993.

Noel, Thomas J. *The City and the Saloon.* Lincoln: University of Nebraska, 1982.

O'Higgins, Harvey, and Ben B. Lindsey. *The Beast.* New York: Doubleday, 1910.

Persico, Joseph, *11/11/11.* New York: Random House, 2004.

Press Syndicate of America. *Press Biographies Representative Men of America.* Denver: Press Syndicate of America, 1906.

Secrest, Clark. *Hell's Belles: Denver's Brides of the Multitudes.* Aurora, Colorado: Hindsight Historical Publications, 1996.

Smiley, Jerome C. *History of Denver.* Denver: Sun Publishing, 1901.

Ubbelohde, Carl, Maxine Benson, and Duane A.

Smith. *A Colorado History*. Boulder: Pruett, 1995.

Vickers, William. *History of the City of Denver, Arapahoe County and Colorado*. Chicago: O. L. Baskin, 1880.

Welty, Susan F. *Look Up and Hope!* New York: Thomas Nelson & Sons, 1961.

Wharton, Junius E. *History of the City of Denver from Its Earliest Settlement to the Present Time*. Denver: Byers & Dailey, 1866.

Whitmore, Julie. *A History of Colorado State Penitentiary 1871–1980*. Cañon City, Colorado: Printing Plus, 1984.

ARTICLES

Abbott, Karen. "Colorado Milestones: 'Little Giant' had big impact on justice." *Rocky Mountain News*, April 20, 1999.

Aguayo, Jose. "Los Betabeleros (The Beetworkers)." *Western Voices*. Golden, Colorado: Fulcrum Publishing, 2004.

Bartley, Nancy. "He Shot the Sheriff." *Pacific Northwest, The Seattle Times magazine*, June 20, 2004.

Cook, Alice Spencer. "The Stormy Career of Ben Lindsey," two-part series. *Empire Magazine,*

The Denver Post, December 2 and 9, 1956.

Fox, Sanford J. "The Early History of the Court." *The Future of Children*. David and Lucile Packard Foundation, nd.

———. "The Early History of the Court." *The Juvenile Court*, Volume 6, Number 3, Winter 1996.

Johnson Bill. "Cutting Juvenile Programs: Save Money Now, Pay for It Later?" *Rocky Mountain News*, March 10, 2004.

King, Laoise. "Colorado Juvenile Court History: The First Hundred Years." *The Colorado Lawyer*, Volume 32, Number 4, April 2003.

Labode, Modupe. "Benjamin Lindsey: Colorado's Little Giant." *Colorado History Now*, Colorado Historical Society, July 2003.

Lindsey, Ben B. "Why Girls Go Wrong." *Ladies Home Journal*, undated, Folder 35, Box 1, Lindsey Collection, Western History Department, Denver Public Library.

———. "Some Experiences in the Juvenile Court of Denver." Campaign for Children. Reprinted from *Charities* magazine, November 7, 1903. Folder 5, Box 1, Ben B. Lindsey Collection, Western History Department, Denver Public Library.

————. "The Beast and the Jungle." *Everybody's Magazine*, October 1909.

Lowe, Peggy. "Juvenile Lifers Decried." *Rocky Mountain News*, February 3, 2005.

Melrose, Frances. "When a Child Killed for Greed." *Rocky Mountain News*, January 23, 1949.

Moffeit, Miles, and Kevin Simpson. "Teen Crime/Adult Time." *The Denver Post*, February 19–22, 2006.

Radelet, Michael L. "Capital Punishment in Colorado: 1859–1972." *University of Colorado Law Review*, Volume 74, Issue 3, Summer 2003.

Rodgers, Frederic. "Judge Ben B. Lindsey and the Colorado Ku Klux Klan." *The Colorado Lawyer*, November 1976.

Shepherd, Robert E. Jr. "The Juvenile Court at 100 Years: A Look Back." *Juvenile Justice*, Volume VI, Number 2, December 1999.

Warren, Jenifer. "For Young Offenders, a Softer Approach." *Los Angeles Times*, February 1, 2005.

Yen, Hope, Associated Press. "No Youth Executions." *Rocky Mountain News*, March 2, 2005.

PAMPHLETS

Biennial Report of the Commissioners of the Colorado State Penitentiary. Denver: Smith Brooks, 1900, 1902, 1904.

Biennial Report of the State Board of Pardons of the State of Colorado. Denver: Smith Brooks, 1904, 1906.

The Denver Juvenile Court, Women's Protective League, Denver, 1913. Folder 67, Box 1, Ben B. Lindsey Collection, Western History Department, Denver Public Library.

Denver Public Schools Hand Book. Denver: Globe Printing Co., December 1912.

Juvenile Justice: A Century of Change. Washington, D.C.: Office of Juvenile Justice and Delinquency Prevention, U.S. Department of Justice, December 1999.

Laws Passed at the Thirteenth Session of the General Assembly of the State of Colorado. Denver: Smith Brooks, 1901.

The Problem of the Children and How the State of Colorado Cares for Them: A Report of the Juvenile Court of Denver, 1904. Denver: The Merchants Publishing Co., 1904.

Report of the Juvenile Division of the County Court of Arapahoe County, Colorado, From January

7, 1901, to July 1, 1902. File 1, Box 1, Ben B. Lindsey Collection, Western History Department, Denver Public Library.

Senate Journal of the General Assembly of the State of Colorado, 13th Session. Denver: Smith Brooks, 1901.

Sixth Biennial Report of the State Board of Charities and Corrections, 1901–1902. Denver: Smith Brooks, 1903.

Twenty-Five Years of the Juvenile and Family Court of Denver, Colorado. Denver: Judge Ben B. Lindsey, 1924.

MANUSCRIPTS AND PAPERS

Colorado State Penitentiary Affairs/Warden C. P. Hoyt's letters, FF-7, Box 26702, Colorado State Archives.

Governor Charles S. Thomas correspondence, January–June 1899. Files 1–4, Box 26700, Colorado State Archives.

Governor Jesse F. McDonald correspondence, executive record, 1905–6. Page 341, Volume 47, Box 8924, Colorado State Archives.

———. outgoing correspondence, June 27, 1905–December 8, 1906. Volume 46, Box 8923, Colorado State Archives.

Penitentiary guard notebook, 1896–99, WH1153, Box 2, Folder 3, Wayne Patterson Collection, Western History Department, Denver Public Library.

"A Prisoner's Story," Pages 28–36, WH1153, Box 2, Folder 23, Wayne Patterson Collection, Western History Department, Denver Public Library.

NEWSPAPERS

Buffalo (New York) *Inquirer*

Cañon City (Colorado) *Clipper*

Cañon City (Colorado) *Times*

The Cañon City (Colorado) *Record*

Cañon City (Colorado) *Daily Record*

The Colorado Sun, Denver

Denver Eye

The Denver Post

The Denver Republican

The Denver Times

Denver Tribune-Republican

The Evening Denver Post

Los Angeles Times

Minneapolis Tribune

Philadelphia North American

Pueblo (Colorado) *Chieftain*

Rocky Mountain News, Denver

Museums and Libraries

Adams County Historical Society Museum, Henderson, Colorado

Battle Creek, Michigan, Historical Society

Colorado Historical Society, Denver

Colorado Prison Museum, Cañon City, Colorado

Colorado State Archives, Denver

Local History Center, Cañon City, Colorado, Library

Mazzulla Collection, Colorado Historical Society, Denver

Newburgh, New York, Historical Society

Special Collections Department, University of Iowa Libraries, Iowa City, Iowa

Western History and Geneaology Department, Denver Public Library

On-Line

Anderson, Diana. "Warden C. P. Hoyt." Local History Center, Cañon City Public Library. http://ccpl.lib.co.us/Prisons.

Colorado Department of Human Services. "Colorado Juvenile Justice System." 2001. www.cs sd11k12.co.us/springcreek/about_us/dye_ colorado_juvenile_justice_system.

Felton, W. B., warden. "Rules for the Government of the Officers and Employees of the Colorado

State Penitentiary." 1881–82. Local History Center, Cañon City Public Library. http://ccpl.lib.co.us/Prisons.

Humes, Edward. "A Brief History of Juvenile Court." www.edwardhumes.com/articles/ juvhist.shtml.

Juvenile Justice InfoCenter. "What Is Juvenile Justice?" www.juvenilejusticecenter.com.

Kresnak, Jack. "Juvenile Court Turns 100, But Is the Party Over?" *Youth Today-Youth Tomorrow*, March 1999. www.ytyt.org/infobank/documnet.cfm/parent/488.

Sherard, Gerald E. "A Short History of the Colorado State Penitentiary." Colorado Department of Personnel & Administration. www.colorado.gov/dpa/doit/archives/pen/history.htm.

Smith, Jack F. "Judge Gilliam." http://100.juvenile law.net/Judges/Gilliam.htm.

U.S. Department of Health and Human Services. "Working with the Courts in Child Protection." 1992. http://nccanch.acf.hhs.gov/pubs/usermanuals/courts/courtsb.cfm.

Courtesy Larry Laszlo/CoMedia

About the Author

Dick Kreck, a columnist for *The Denver Post*, is an amateur historian who moved to Colorado from California in 1968, thus beating the rush. A graduate of San Francisco State College, he worked at the *San Francisco Examiner* and the *Los Angeles Times* before joining *The Post*. His previous books are *Denver in Flames: Forging a New Mile High City* and the best-selling *Murder at the Brown Palace: A True Story of Seduction and Betrayal*. He lives in Denver.

Also by Dick Kreck:

Murder at the Brown Palace

Thirty weeks on the best-seller list!

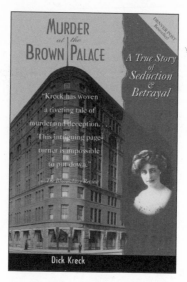

A true story of crime and passion, *Murder at the Brown Palace* brings to life one of the most notorious murders in Denver's history. This gripping tale, which begins in 1911 in Denver's grand old hotel, involves seduction, betrayal, murder, and mayhem. A love story, mystery, and courtroom drama all wrapped into one.

"Kreck has woven a riveting tale of murder and deception. ... This intriguing page-turner is impossible to put down."
—*The Bloomsbury Review*

Fulcrum Publishing
16100 Table Mountain Parkway, Suite 300, Golden, CO 80403
To order call (800) 992-2908 or visit www.fulcrumbooks.com.
Also available at your local bookstore.